Praise for
Boy Wonders

"The quirky, must-read *Gl...* ...s
to both the boy and the wond... -
multi-faceted, colourful, pol... *Boy Wonders* is
terrific, a book you should buy, read once for the pleasure, read
again for the craft and then . . . give it to a twelve-year-old."

—*Winnipeg Free Press*

"Cathal Kelly's reporting (for this newspaper) about sports is so
entertaining that even if (like this reader) you don't much care
about sports, you may regularly read him anyway. His debut
memoir, *Boy Wonders*, about growing up in the 1970s and 80s,
promises to be emotional, funny and packed full with nerdy
obsessions and ill-advised fashion choices. Also sports."

—*The Globe and Mail*

"Cathal Kelly has the gift only first-rate writers have: he knows
which obsessions matter most, however much the rest of the
world pretends they don't. The result, in *Boy Wonders*, is a breath-
taking portrait of a boy's inner life: lonely, clueless, hilarious,
and full to the brim with every variety of passion. You will be
glad you read it, whoever you are."

—Ian Brown, author of *Sixty*

"This is the book you should be reading if you want to know
how complicated boys become grown men. It's not riddled with
rules, just gem-like stories, each a beautifully crafted revelation.

Whether he's writing about first kisses, pop-culture fandom, broken families or the ambiguities of faith, Kelly masterfully balances the hilarious with the heartbreaking, sometimes in a single sentence. A coming-of-age classic."

—Lisa Gabriele, author of *The Winters*

"What a wondrous treat this book is. Looking back at his childhood, Cathal Kelly takes things that we all recognize—subway trains, Michael Jackson's jacket, bickering families—and spins them into a fascinating and heart-rending web of life and memory. I've always wondered about boys; this book provides many answers, and much pleasure."

—Elizabeth Renzetti, author of *Shrewed*

BOY WONDERS

A MEMOIR OF CHILDHOOD, OBSESSION AND GROWING UP

CATHAL

KELLY

Anchor Canada

Portions of "*Star Wars*" and "The Church" were previously published in a different
form in *The Globe and Mail*.

Library and Archives Canada Cataloguing in Publication

Kelly, Cathal, author
    Boy wonders / Cathal Kelly.

ISBN 978-0-385-68750-8 (softcover)
Ebook ISBN 978-0-385-68749-2

    1. Kelly, Cathal--Childhood and youth. 2. Sportswriters--
Canada--Biography. 3. Popular culture. 4. Autobiographies.
I. Title.

GV742.42.K45A3 2019   070.4'49796092   C2018-901709-0

Cover image: P_Wei/Getty Images

Printed and bound in Canada

Published in Canada by Anchor Canada,
a division of Penguin Random House Canada Limited,
a Penguin Random House Company

www.penguinrandomhouse.ca

10 9 8 7 6 5 4 3 2 1

Penguin
Random House
ANCHOR CANADA

For Margaret

CONTENTS

INTRODUCTION

I WAS ALMOST NINE YEARS OLD when I began digging the hole. I picked a spot near the rear of our backyard, in a flower bed hard up against the neighbour's chain-link fence. Since nothing grew there anyway, it seemed like a good spot for renovation.

A good deal of my life up until that point had been spent obsessing about machines that excavated—backhoes, tractors, snowplows. Just about any sort of large truck thrilled me. The power of them, these tools of transformation.

I also liked the idea that if anybody got in your way, you could just run them over. If you had a truck, you were free to do as you liked. The hole was an extension of this desire. I started it with an old metal Tonka toy that operated as a minia-ture gravel mover. That got me nowhere fast. Then I switched to one of my mother's garden tools. That was equally useless. Eventually, I found a shovel buried under a pile of junk in the garage and began making some serious progress.

I can't say how many days I spent on the hole. It seems like dozens, but at that age time accordions inward. A day is like a week, a week like a month. I did spend a good long time on the hole. Longer than I'd ever spent on any one project.

It was tough going at first, but once through the toughened top layer, the earth got sandy. After a couple of days, I was planted inside the hole, up to my knees.

Every so often, my younger brother, Brendan, would come out to inspect the work. He wanted very badly to participate, but this was my hole. After a short argument, Brendan wandered off to dig his own hole. Since digging a hole is a ridiculous thing to do, he soon lost interest. From then on, he settled on coming out into the backyard to annoy me for hours at a time by throwing a baseball against the back wall of the garage. The wall was wooden and the ball had no bounce, it would only drop to the ground directly in front of the garage. He'd have to run over and fetch it each time. It was an even stupider thing to do than digging a hole, though, in retrospect, a telling insight into our brotherly relations.

My mother showed no interest in the hole until the neighbours complained. (God, how our neighbours suffered over the years.) They worried that my hole would collapse a portion of their immaculately kept garden. It is a potent Irishism that no one should presume to tell you what you can or can't do on your own land. My mother was now suddenly pro-hole.

I began buttressing my hole with boards I found in (or stole from) the laneway behind the garage. Everything a kid needed was in that laneway—bricks, bottles, stones. All the detritus that can be used to build or destroy—the two polarities of the boyhood imagination.

The biggest problem was what to do with all the excess dirt. I could dig for a while, tossing it out behind me. But then I'd have to get out and re-shovel the pile to a point where it wasn't slipping back in. Eventually, I was spending most of my time moving the pile farther and farther away. That slowed me down.

After a few days, I was ready to show the hole to people. Friends would come over and nod approvingly at its width and depth—about the size around of a manhole cover and maybe four or five feet deep.

"How far will the hole go?" they asked.

I wasn't sure. Once you've gone to the trouble of starting a hole, you don't want to limit yourself.

After the sandy bit, the earth got hard again, loamy and compact. There were roots to cut through—emanating from where, I couldn't say. The nearest tree was thirty feet away. Working only with the strength of a child and a steak knife filched from the kitchen took forever. Eventually, I was right down there in the hole, though I could still get my elbows up on the edges and pull myself out. I considered expanding the hole. Maybe I could enlarge it to the size of a grave? But that would mean ruining the grass. There was nowhere to go but down.

One night, my mother asked me if I was going to China. The question annoyed me because she knew I knew all about the Earth's molten core. But I said yes, sure, China, why not?

One day I really got at it. It must've been hours of digging. After a while, I could no longer hear the noise of the neighbourhood. No cars passing or birdsong. I was working with a trowel, smoothing the sides and rearranging the boards. After the day's work was done, I tossed out the trowel and reached up to grab the sides. They had grown beyond my grasp. I was perhaps five feet tall, and the hole was close to seven.

I tried planting my feet against the walls of the hole and propelling myself upward. That didn't work. There was no purchase there. I straightened my back against one wall and tried running up the other. That worked just well enough to allow me to fall back down into the hole from a height several times. I called out once or twice, but stopped because I had at the time a strong fear of seeming foolish. I did not want a stranger to find me in a trap of my own idiotic design.

I ran through the scenarios.

What if no one found me? Unlikely.

What if it rained? I'd float to the top.

What if I had to go to the bathroom? Dirt is very absorbent.

What if the hole collapsed? Not my hole. This was a hole built with quality in mind.

So I sat down in the hole to wait. That's what I remember best.

Memories are strange things. Think back on the fondest recollections of your distant past. Usually, the memory is reassuring and warm. In all likelihood, it's remarkably detailed. Coming down the stairs on Christmas morning or that thing your father explained to you on that long drive to wherever, something that's always stuck with you and helped to orient your relationship with him. These remembrances seem almost too real to be credited.

Freud would say that's because they are. He called them "screen memories"—several disparate impressions, often unconnected, pastiched by your mind into one powerful recollection that covers over all the others. In the process, negative feeling is removed.

It's a powerful tool of the brain, meant to comfort us.

By Freud's lights, screen memories often have a negative function, compelling us to repeat in adulthood those anti-social behaviours we observed as children. Maybe your father was screaming at you during that drive, rather than talking to you. Maybe you've become a screamer. Maybe you can't bear to be around screaming. Maybe you've figured out the difference between what you think happened and what did and found a way through it. And maybe it actually happened the way you remember. Your father's gone. Who's to say?

Everything that follows here is not necessarily exactly as it happened, but exactly as I remember it happening. I've seen *Rashomon* enough times to know there's a profound difference.

But at our core, what are we but an agglomeration of the things we *believe* happened to us? Reality has very little to do with it. So I remember being in the hole. I remember it better than yesterday or the day before. I still dream about it. Those few times I have trod across a freshly plowed field, the smell transports me back there.

It was cool in the hole, and utterly still. It was soundless, but it did not have that same quality as the silence you feel when you cover your ears. It was wide-open in its emptiness. What I felt there was safety. I was hidden away and could not be disturbed or impeded by any person or force. I felt calm. My thoughts were liquid and ordered at the same time. I wasn't thinking about the hole or why I'd done it or how I'd got there. I wasn't thinking at all. It's only in childhood that we can have purpose without an end. A child at play has no objectives or goals. We do in order to do. Taking religiosity out of it, it was the first time I felt whatever people mean when they say the word *Zen*.

Like so many other insignificant happenings of childhood, that one has defined me. As an adult, I have strong mole-like tendencies. I like to be tucked up in small places, as long as the exit is open. If I get into a bed that is pushed against a wall, I cannot sleep unless my back is touching it. When I enter a room, I move to its rear and put objects—a table, a bar—in between the crowd and myself. I like to watch what's happening at the party through that aperture, however haphazard.

I was in there a while. Maybe an hour. Maybe two. I wasn't bothered, and so kept no track of time. When I heard my mother's voice out in the yard, it wasn't an interruption. My moment of profound, aimless introspection simply stopped, and the buzzing in my brain kicked up again, like an engine turning over.

"Here," I said. "I'm here."

She wandered over and looked into the hole. "Are you finished?"

"Yes. Can you help me out?"

My mother is not a big person and, even then, I was. She lay down at the edge and I got hold of the arms of her shirt and scuffled up the sides until we were able to wrestle me to the top. She was as filthy as I by the end of this process, and more than a little put out. Annoying the buttinsky neighbours was good and all, but it was she who had to do the laundry.

"I think that's enough digging," she said. My mother never said I couldn't do things. She only suggested it in a way that had more force than any order.

I didn't argue. The hole had achieved its purpose. The next day I filled it in. There was a sizable excess of dirt left afterward, which I believed to be meaningful, but could not say why.

From then on I would think of everything I did, every exploration, every falling down the wormhole of a new obsession, every occasion that seemed a portent of something more important than itself in the terms of digging that hole. That's what we do in life—we dig. Occasionally, we get somewhere, discover some small treasure. More often, the hole collapses in on us. Or we fill it in. And then we dig again.

WE LEFT THAT HOUSE when I was fourteen years old. It was an ugly, aluminum-sided bungalow, conspicuously out of place in a working-class west-end Toronto neighbourhood filled with two-storey brick homes. We'd spent six or seven years there. We lived in many spots throughout my childhood, but if you ask me which one was home, that was it.

I went back there recently. It's only twenty minutes across town, but I hadn't been there in years. In order to get to it, I passed what had been my father's house, around the corner and a block down the street.

Though the same in every general way, the neighbourhood has changed in every important way in thirty years. Become expensive and moved up the class ladder. It isn't quite as Maltese and Italian. The frontages are spiffier. The trees have grown. All the spots I knew are gone or replaced.

My home is much as it was, though freshly painted. I snuck up the driveway on a weekday afternoon to peek into the backyard. They've refurbished the deck and the garage. The cherry tree is gone. It's foreign territory now. In the spot where there was once a hole, someone has planted a large, opulent bush of some sort, the sort that takes a long while to come in.

But in my mind, I know the hole is still there. Because I dug it.

As life goes on, digging seems less momentous because it has become a habit. Somewhere between ten and twenty, you stop digging for its own sake and begin digging for something specific—a job, a relationship, money, admiration, an escape. Like your perception of time, once you cross over from one to the other, there is no going back. All that remains is the echo of how it once felt, and a nostalgia for those careless times.

STAR WARS

TWO MOVIES STICK IN MY MIND from the summer of 1980. The less important of them was *Ordinary People*.

My parents had recently split up. I was now spending weekends with my father, a man of few fixations. The only extracurriculars I remember him enjoying were the odd bit of hockey watching and long hours spent sitting in an easy chair listening to John Prine at skull-cracking volume. Years later, I'd work a Prine concert and nearly convulse during the first bars of "Sam Stone."

When my father did settle on something, it was intensely important that it be followed up on immediately. One day, having never before shown any interest in what I did in school, he decided to teach me algebra. At the time, I was still struggling through multiplication tables. I sat down with him suspiciously. He took out a textbook he'd acquired from God knows where. There was a long preamble that involved saying, "This stuff is easy" many times over. "If x equals 2 and y equals 3, then what is z?" he asked, jabbing at the numbers on the page as if that might make them more comprehensible.

Blank look from me. More jabbing from him. Silence. Further jabbing. Now sighing. Mounting frustration, which I knew from experience would soon become rage. When I asked why x instead of, say, a or g or r, he got up, flung the book across the table and left the room. He never mentioned algebra again.

I still don't understand why it can't be a or g or r and think of it as a small revenge that I will never know.

All that to say that when my parents were together my father did very few things with us. Nothing, actually. But now that he was on his own, he felt pressure to engage in cultural activities with his children. Of course, they were always the sort of thing he thought he might like, rather than anything we liked. Aggressively so.

This is how I came to be sitting in a theatre on a Saturday afternoon at eight years old watching *Ordinary People*. Because he could neither drink nor smoke, my father fidgeted through the entirety of a two-hour movie particularly unsuited to children. The plotline involved a frigid mother, her gentle, wronged husband and a son who cannot forgive himself for having driven them apart. Even as a kid, I thought it rather too on the nose.

My father wept at the end and I ate myself sick on popcorn. Neither of us left the theatre feeling enlightened. I was already beginning to miss my old father—the one who had no interest in things or in doing any of them with me.

What truly pained me about the experience was that I had very specifically told him what I wanted to see—*The Empire Strikes Back*.

"Haven't you already seen that?" he said.

"Yes, but what does . . ."

"Then forget it."

While we sat upstairs at the Runnymede Theatre suffering through one of our intermittent attempts at bonding, I could occasionally hear an explosion or laser blast from the downstairs showing of the *Star Wars* sequel. Oh, the humanity.

Like everyone else in my generation, *Star Wars* was not just one of my interests. It was a singular obsession. If you were a kid in the late seventies, *Star Wars* was Jonestown with a marketing arm.

I had seen *The Empire Strikes Back* earlier in the summer with my mother. In its own way, that had also been a painful experience. There had been an unbearable buildup to that excursion. I'm not sure when I heard that *Star Wars* would have a sequel (the term was not yet in common parlance—we just thought of it as "another"). Word got to us through the schoolyard telephone. This was the blissful time of life when you were forewarned of nothing—things just happened and you heard about them afterward. So this was a precious piece of advance intelligence.

Of course, you couldn't trust kids. Kids talked all sorts of nonsense. Another *Star Wars*? I mean, they'd already wrapped that thing up, hadn't they? What else were these people going to do, blow up another planet? (This is, I assume, how Hollywood works—think like a seven-year-old.) After hearing about *Star Wars II*, I fled school like an animal to seek confirmation. When an adult told me that, yes, it was true, I felt a very-close-to-hallucinogenic level of joy.

From that point, time worked to two points of a vector—the right now and the whenever-the-next-*Star-Wars*-arrived. It may have been weeks. It felt like years. The in-between was unbearably sweet. Life had its purpose.

Everything pulls back into focus on a Bloor Street sidewalk outside the Runnymede Theatre waiting to be let into an afternoon showing of *The Empire Strikes Back*.

The first part of this memory is muddy. I recall the sense of pant-wetting anticipation. I remember seeing the poster pinned up alongside the doorway—the first tangible evidence that this was really happening. Mostly, I was disoriented by expectation. I felt sure this experience was going to change my life for the better. I was going to get some answers to important questions.

Then the van appeared. I remember the van quite specifically. It was brown, an old American beater, windowless with a sliding panel on the right side. It was moving very slowly down the lineup, eastward along Bloor. The panel was open and someone—a man, maybe a teenager—was leaning out the door dangerously. He was yelling something at everyone.

The line stretched along the street for hundreds of feet, and we were standing up near the front. As the van finally crept within shouting distance, the guy leaning out the door screamed, "Darth Vader is Luke's father! Darth Vader is Luke's father!"

Then the van peeled off on its way back to hell.

For a thoughtful moment, no one said anything. Most of the people in line were grown-ups. They were quietly weighing the evidence for and against.

Then a whole bunch of people groaned at once. Not normal groaning. The bad, painful sort. Soon, people were hopping up and down on the sidewalk. Like, actually hopping. Punching the air. People were freaking out.

In what may have been the most cinematic moment of my life, I asked my mother, "Is it true? Is Darth Vader Luke's father?"

My mother was at *Star Wars* on sufferance. She shrugged. I

began to suspect that she had no idea who Darth Vader was. Everything was darkening.

A few minutes later, sitting in the theatre, this movie should have been changing everything for me, frame by frame. I had not seen any of these people—people I felt like I knew—for years. But I couldn't appreciate it in the moment. Not even the Tauntauns. I sat there waiting to find out if Van Man was telling us the truth.

We got to the climax. Darth Vader is knocking the crap out of Luke in the bowels of Cloud City. He gets him out onto a parapet—"You are beaten. It is useless to resist." He chops off Luke's hand.

In this moment, I thought, "Good. He lied."

And then, after a bit of to and fro, Darth Vader says, "No, I am your father."

Jesus Christ, the disappointment. His father? What a goddamned cheat.

I left the joint in a rage. My mother was also in foul humour, but only because she'd been forced to watch a bunch of dim-wittery about spaceships and men in capes for two hours.

The author Colin Wilson describes real pleasure as existing in two states simultaneously. While you're being warmed in your chair by the fire, a part of you is standing in the snowstorm outside. It's the combination that gives you true satisfaction.

I wouldn't read Wilson for years, but when I did, I recognized the theory. I've lived it many times in reverse. While unable to enjoy what should have been the most world-altering news of my life, I could still picture how incredible it would have felt had I not known it was coming. In the moment, there was an unbearable sense of having been cheated.

My life, the way I thought about it and quite possibly the way I chose to live it, turned slightly after the van passed by. Through no real fault of its own, *Star Wars* had turned me into a cynic at seven years old.

I assume everyone of a certain age has their own reasons for, and their own way of, being consumed by *Star Wars*. What gave it real potency was that the entire exercise was, by necessity, imaginative. This wasn't a book or a piece of music that could be pored over again and again. As art, *Star Wars* was more of a happening—you went to the theatre, saw it once and then did not see it again. Nobody in my family was going to get dragged back to watch the same movie twice. My father wouldn't even stoop to seeing it once.

There were written materials as reference points, but none that I had access to. I spent my allowance on comic books down the block at Mike's Convenience. Mike made very little effort to stay on the cutting edge of popular culture. If it wasn't at Mike's, it didn't exist for me.

And so soon after I'd seen it for the first time, *Star Wars* quickly bled away as a coherent narrative, becoming the mere suggestion of one. You could put together the building blocks of how it went—unhappy teenager; evil Empire; old hermit; magic; spaceships; Rebel Alliance; crushed in a trash compactor; escape the trash compactor!; swordfight; things look bad; one last chance; unhappy teenager blows up ersatz planet through inexplicable design flaw; everyone gets a medal, except the ape.

But the details were fuzzy. Remember when Ben scared off the Sand People? What did the Sand People look like exactly? Unless you had the action figure, you weren't sure. This made it imperative to get that action figure.

Before the wretched prequels came out in the late nineties, George Lucas had already made billions for himself licensing *Star Wars* toys. That's because, for most children, the only way to see the movie again was to restage it in their home. Lucas's greatest achievement is that he forced an entire generation to become pipsqueak auteurs.

Re-enactments required a critical mass of figures that, given logistical and financial impediments particular to childhood, was impossible to achieve.

My mother couldn't understand why one storm trooper action figure wasn't enough.

But you needed multiple storm troopers to do the thing properly. I begged for them. Begged. No dice.

There were almighty rows on the subject of action figures, on how they might be procured and in what quantities. I considered stealing the money I needed, but it's not like I could swan into a department store on my own and buy them. My mother would have to take me. And had I then sashayed up to the till and produced a wad of bills from my pocket, it would have prompted uncomfortable questions.

So I dragooned in other figures to act as undercover/traitorous/triple-agent storm troopers. It was a first effort at post-modernism. It didn't hang together very well.

Eventually, I gave up trying to recreate Lucas's vision. Instead, I built my own.

A great deal has been written about why *Star Wars* is so effective (most of which I've taken pains to avoid). Its point of access is Shakespearean—the film appeals everywhere to everyone. In creating the movies, Lucas researched the structure of various world mythologies. He used the commonalities as a road map when writing *Star Wars*. That's one explanation.

I think there's another as well—that *Star Wars* presented an alternate, irresistible idea of family.

At the outset, every one of the main characters is terrifyingly isolated. Princess Leia is captured and her planet destroyed. We never see any of her people again. Luke's family is murdered. The droids—only one of whom can speak—are forgotten trash. Obi-Wan Kenobi lives by himself in a cave. Fleeing assassins, all Han Solo has is a talking pet. Every major new character—the good guys, at least—lives this way. Lando is miserably trying to convince himself he's not wasting his life on a floating gas mine. Yoda has a whole planet to spread out on, and he lives in a mud igloo the size of a horizontal hall closet. None of these people have friends, or any that we're shown. They are adrift in the universe until they find each other.

Underneath the Western tropes, every major scene in the films emphasizes this bond between misfits. All of Lucas's best dialogue—and there isn't much of it—revolves around the gentle (or ungentle) teasing we can only inflict on people we love.

Once they find each other, everything is possible. They can even blow up metal Pluto through an airshaft.

Lightsabers and hyperspace are not *Star Wars*'s most affecting fantasy. This is. That no matter how out of place or set upon you feel in the world, there is somewhere you belong and people you belong with.

Star Wars isn't really sci-fi or action or a hybrid of the two. It's a love story. Entirely platonic, though in the true sense of that word—something quite passionate, only lacking an element of the sensual. Something deep and abiding. You don't think of it this way as a child, but the message is powerful enough to seep through. That this is what love is meant to look and sound like. Eventually, I constructed a *Star Wars* that revolved entirely around me. I was the main character. Obi-Wan was my teacher. Han Solo was my older brother. I had a vivid running daydream of learning to speak Wookiee. I didn't care for Luke because he was breathing my air. I didn't want to be him. Luke was the feckless, needy child—just like me. I wanted to eliminate him and take his place. I never owned a Luke Skywalker action figure.

The effect of this was heightened by the emotional precariousness of my life in that moment. After the divorce, my mother was forced to move in with her brother. We occupied the upper floor of his house. She'd fled the marriage, leaving us with no cash reserves. Suddenly, she was working all hours, often late into the night.

We were all very aware of the imposition on my uncle and his family. Beyond making no trouble, we tried to be invisible.

I brought Brendan, then three years old, home from the babysitter's. I made us dinner. I put us both to bed. My mother would arrive after we were already asleep.

My brother was an unusually quiet and contemplative child. Almost eerily so. You'd ask Brendan a question and he'd turn to look at you for a long time. Then he'd arch his eyebrows and turn away again without replying.

His babysitter, Mrs. Spiteri, was Maltese. She and her family—an enormously warm and tightknit group, essentially our complete opposites—were the sort of immigrants who'd created a simulacrum of the old country in their home. They raised rabbits; cooked the traditional foods; did the traditional things; and spoke nothing but their native language. Brendan spent so much time in their company, and so little in ours, that he didn't fully understand English. In order to summon him, my mother learned to say *"Ejja l'hawn"*—Maltese for "Come here." I imagine he thought the Spiteris were his real family, and my mother and I the people with whom he inexplicably had to spend the evenings. He often got this look when I showed up to collect him, an "Oh Jesus, not this guy again" sort of expression. But he was an agreeable kid and he always came without a fuss.

With Brendan functionally incommunicado and my mother gone, I was left with many hours alone inside my own head. The majority of them were devoted to the construction of *Star Wars*–based narratives. I don't recall being lonely, as such. There were always people around. I just didn't bother speaking to any of them. What I did feel was unsettled. Those *Star Wars* fantasies bulwarked a vital sense that everything would turn out okay. They convinced me that "right now" didn't matter.

How many years had Obi-Wan spent in the cave, or Han Solo on the run? When you're seven or nine or eleven, what's a year? It's forever. At that age, time has no meaning. *Star Wars* gave me hope that at some indeterminate future point it would all turn out fine. I would eventually find that strange family that understood me. I would have company and people to talk to and perhaps to even care about me.

None of this would have worked if I'd had full access to the films or the supporting canon. Had I been able to refer back to exactly how it had gone down or, worse yet, read books that went beyond the universe of the films, my fantasy would have collapsed under the imposition of order. I needed it fluid, organic and responsive to what was happening in my life. As I changed, *Star Wars* changed to suit me.

I suspect that like a lot of kids born in the sixties and seventies, I used the half-forgotten memory of those films—the first two in particular—as a blunt, therapeutic tool.

After the disappointment of *Empire*, Darth Vader worked his way to the front of my bedroom recreations. In *Star Wars*, he is a cartoon. In *Empire*, he's a tragic hero.

He's also a murderous sociopath, but Vader was the one character who showed you how much he cared. Obi-Wan was too stiff, Han too glib, Leia too haughty. Presumably like their creator, all of Lucas's projections were afraid of their feelings.

Vader was all feeling (which Lucas and his proxies priggishly presented as a flaw). He'd lost his son, and he wanted him back. He wanted that so badly he'd eventually allow himself to be killed to make it happen.

If every son spends his life wanting to be seen—really seen—by his father, and vice versa, Vader was the exemplar of that urge. Is there any line more plaintive or searching in the trilogy than Vader's desperate "If you only knew the power of the Dark Side"—and especially the way James Earl Jones draws out the crucial word? That moment was the closest *Star Wars* got to a cathedral ceiling.

I began to focus exclusively on that scene, which I'd hated on first viewing. In the months after *Empire* was released, it was everywhere. "I am your father" became a catchphrase and then a joke. It was the one part of the movies you could watch again. There was something unspeakably powerful about that outstretched hand, and the way Vader balled his fist as he said, "Join me, and together we can rule the galaxy as father and son."

That line of dialogue coloured all of my interactions with my father. Now that he was alone, he was slipping further into an alcoholic haze. My ur-image of him at that time is of a man planted on a couch in the living room of his new house, a rum and Diet Coke in one hand and a butt in the other. He'd spend whole days like that. Eventually, I began to bring him food. When I would return a week later, none of it would have been eaten. Once, he took me out for pie. As we left the diner, he threw up on the sidewalk while I stood there, embarrassed and repulsed. It was the first thing he'd had to eat in days and his stomach rejected its richness. I don't know how he lived as long as he did. This was not someone who could rule the galaxy with you.

In the movie, Luke (foolishly) declines the offer.

In my dreams, I always said "Yes."

I'd play out all the ways we'd take over the galaxy—who would get it first, what we'd wear and how he'd make it up to me for cutting off my hand (which, magnanimously, I wouldn't make a big deal about). I didn't fear evil, because I had no idea what that looked like. But I was afraid of being alone and unwanted. Vader was the cure for that. We had many long, important conversations in my head.

Vader was the most important fictional character in my life, and I knew him better than some real people who should have been him for me.

Eventually, working in tandem, Lucas and I would ruin all of this. Lucas pooched it in *Return of the Jedi*. The allegory of family was now being presented in maudlin, indiscriminate fashion. They'd let anyone in, including the goddamned Ewoks. Vader dies. Luke eats his cake and has it too, winning the war and reuniting with the old man. The core failure of *Jedi* is that there is no sacrifice by the victors. This was the world reduced to gauzy holograms and an absence of complications. *Star Wars* no longer seemed anything like messy, real life.

I ruined it for myself by getting older and buying the movies on VHS cassette.

Freed to watch them whenever I wanted, I did so compulsively. They became a comforting talisman or an emotional crutch, depending on how you want to look at it.

Have a bad day? Go down to the basement and watch *Star Wars*. Watch all three in a row. Memorize the dialogue. Get totally lost in it, but without any sort of rigour or inventiveness. Become a receptacle instead of whatever fills it. I lost hold of my version of the *Star Wars* world and replaced it with Lucas's. I no longer remember most of the games I used to play or the alternative storylines I made up. I'd stopped being the creator.

Years later, Lucas released the first of the prequels. On Day 1, I was back in line again, up at the front.

Star Wars made me cynical, but apparently not cynical enough. Even Lucas's need to fiddle with the epic world he'd made through tedious expansion can't spoil *Star Wars*. For those of us lucky enough to be young at the beginning, it's already threaded through our imaginations. What Greek myths were to generations, *Star Wars* is to just one. Resenting what it's become is like raging at the religion you were raised in—you may fundamentally disagree with it, but it's another thing to separate yourself from the shelter of that framework.

In line for the first prequel, I retold the story of the van to the people I was with. I've dined out on it for ages. It's lost all of its sad, thwarted edge. It's just funny now.

One of the inevitable processes of growing older is that all of your disappointments are compounded geologically, compressed one on top of another into an indiscriminate layer cake of experience. They hurt less individually and mean less as a whole. Eventually, you realize this isn't a good or bad thing. It just is. *Star Wars* taught me that, too.

PORNO

MY FIRST DIVE INTO PORNOGRAPHY was a pleasant accident. During one of my comic book runs—*The Amazing Spider-Man*; *Shang-Chi: Master of Kung Fu*; *Conan the Barbarian*—I dropped a copy of *Heavy Metal* on the pile. The cover featured a guy in a loincloth killing a giant snake. Oversized reptiles were a bigger deal in the eighties—plainly a Reagan metaphor.

I was a particular admirer of Conan. In one of his crossovers with mainstream Marvel characters, he's dropped into modern times with no clue of how to get along. He takes to robbing people. He rolls a pizza delivery guy (one panel showed him eating pizza with one hand while holding the poor schmuck up by the lapels with the other). Instead of keeping the bills, Conan tosses them, preferring the heft of coins. This struck me as a blinding insight into the under-considered aspects of barbarian time travel.

It was its similarity to *Conan* that drew me to *Heavy Metal*—which is a mélange of sword-and-sorcerer fantasy, space opera and soft porn.

The first nude woman I came across in its pages didn't quite register. The second one did. All the women in *Heavy Metal* are—this is meta—cartoons of cartoons. Insanely proportioned, always unclothed and uniformly lascivious.

I was about seven years old. A rolling ticker began to scroll in my mind: "THIS IS SEX . . . SEX . . . SEX . . . MORE TO COME AS DETAILS EMERGE."

I was lying in bed. I pulled the comic in closer to my body until I was lying on top of it, in case someone walked in. Everything about this was wrong and, worse than that, shameful. When I thought of women as a group—and this would not include members of my family, who were functionally genderless to me—my only reference point was my teachers. I could not conceive of them acting in this way (with or without giant snakes). I would have found it easier to believe that Ms. Sullivan or Ms. Florio were undercover astronauts than people who had ever had sex.

I did know about sex. It was one of many things I'd pestered my mother about until she got me a book on the topic. Whenever I wondered long or loudly enough about anything, a book would appear. If someone had put together a compendium called *Life: Here's How It Works*, my mother would've set it a place at dinner and told me to make my enquiries in that direction.

The sex book was *Where Did I Come From?*, a treacly classic about the boundless beauty of making love. It reads now like *Hustler* run through a Vatican editorial board. My mother brought it home one day in a brown paper bag, handed it to me and then pivoted quickly away. Nothing was said. The book was briefly thrilling but, despite the inoffensive nudity, ultimately unsatisfying. I'd figured out most of what was in there for myself. The only mystery that remained was the orgasm, therein described as "a tickly feeling" leading to a "really big sneeze."

I spent a few bad minutes in the kitchen aggressively shoving pepper up my nose to induce sneezing. The experiment resulted in zero sneezing and a great deal of mess that was difficult to explain. In my mind, "tickling" was synonymous with feathers. Feathers were devices specifically designed for tickling. But it is nearly impossible to lay your hands on a good, big feather when you are seven. What I needed was an eagle feather. The only birds I had good access to were pigeons. I tried tickling my own stomach—not entirely unpleasant—but that felt weird. And the book was pretty clear that it had to be someone else holding the feather. I didn't think my friends in grade two would be quite that open-minded.

Suffice to say that I understood sexual mechanics, but not the impulse or the attraction. *Where Did I Come From?* portrayed sex as serious business undertaken by serious people for serious reasons resulting in extremely serious consequences. I put sex aside for the time being to concentrate on my studies. Of dinosaurs.

But now here was *Heavy Metal* prompting a reconsideration. Clearly, something bad was happening here. Good bad. I kept *Heavy Metal* under my mattress. This wasn't exactly CIA-level tradecraft. The concept of "hidden in plain sight" did not occur to me.

At night, after my brother had fallen asleep, I'd sneak the magazine into bed and pore over the naughtiest bits. It got old fast. Very quickly, I required new stimulation.

In a time before the ubiquity of the supermarket, we bought our comestibles down the corner at Mike's Milk & Smokes (even back then, an odd marketing combo).

Mike's was run by someone I assumed was Mike, though I never bothered to ask. He was a taciturn Korean gentleman who insisted that I could not purchase cigarettes for my parents without a note. He might've been 30 or 50 or 110. I was no judge of ages. Though I was in there at least once every day and Mike was the only person I can recall ever being behind the counter, he never gave any indication that he recognized me. Ours was a purely transactional relationship.

Mike's was a claustrophobic place—windows blacked out with du Maurier posters, low ceilinged, overcrowded with shelving. Even as a kid, I had to turn sideways to inch my way toward the fridge at the back.

The magazine rack was directly to your left inside the door. Mike stood guard behind the counter about six feet away, but his view was partially blocked by a gum rack.

I was in there constantly sifting through his meagre selection of comics. Essentially, if Mike stocked it, I'd buy it. Though we weren't close, Mike and I had some fun times together. We particularly enjoyed playing a game called "Are you buying that? No? Then put it down." I'd put the comic down and wait for someone to distract Mike with a purchase. Then I'd pick up another comic and we'd start again.

There were three shelves to the magazine rack. The top one contained the nudie mags. They were out in plain sight and there were a lot of them. The titles meant nothing to me. I knew I could go up there without setting off alarms because that's how I'd got hold of *Heavy Metal* in the first place. I spent a lot of time thinking about how I was going to acquire something more substantive. From a research perspective.

I first considered buying a magazine, but it didn't seem wise to sashay up to the counter with a copy of *Juggs* and a packet of Big League Chew. I could stuff it into a pile of G-rated comics and hope Mike wasn't paying close attention. Except that Mike was always paying close attention.

So it would be theft.

I'd never stolen anything before and I don't have a criminal bent of mind. When crossing over the line to the dark side, it's important to know your skill set.

Even then I knew I was not particularly cunning or good under duress.

I realized that the most important thing I'd need was a distraction. I enlisted my friend Kevin in the scheme. Kevin wasn't very enthusiastic ("Sure"), but he seemed like a cool-under-pressure type.

I would go into Mike's. If Mike wasn't behind the counter (and Mike was always behind the counter), it'd be a snatch-and-grab. If he was there, I would mosey casually to the magazines. Kevin would come in shortly thereafter and buy something (with money I'd provided—a key sweetener to the deal). While Kevin was making his purchase, I would pull the heist.

I obsessed over this operation for days. There were many abortive attempts. A store that was always empty seemed suddenly to be pulling in all sorts of street traffic. It was a regular milk/smokes convention at Mike's.

Kevin started to lose what little enthusiasm he'd had. My window was closing.

Then one day after school, the magic hour arrived. Mike was behind the counter, but no one else was there. I slid into place. Kevin came in behind me, talking very loudly in a preposterously suspicious manner.

"DO YOU HAVE GUM?" he screamed at Mike, while standing directly beside the gum.

"OH. THERE IT IS."

Pause.

"MAYBE I NEED SOMETHING ELSE."

Pause.

"WHAT ELSE DO YOU HAVE?"

This was some shit distraction work. But I was committed now. I reached up blindly and snatched a magazine from the porno rack. Then I dropped it on the ground. Then I picked it up. Then, with some difficulty, I wedged it down the front of my jeans (as a general rule, thieves should wear track pants). That took ages. Then I bolted for the door in such panic that I pulled it into my own face. Once outside, I stood there on the sidewalk, waiting for Kevin to emerge so that we could flee on our getaway vehicles (i.e., bikes).

Five seconds. Ten seconds. Thirty seconds. A minute. Two minutes. Forever.

When Kevin finally emerged, he was in no hurry. He was pulling the top off a freezie with his teeth.

"We should go," I said, gulping air.

"He knows you took it," Kevin said.

"What?"

"He saw you steal the magazine. He said so."

"WHAT?"

"He said that you should bring it back."

"WHAT?!"

Kevin was quite calm about the whole thing. (Where had that guy been when I needed him?) I was in a state of emotional collapse. Oh God, what now? What if Mike came out?

What would he do? Collar me? Call the cops? I could not even bring myself to contemplate the idea that he might tell my mother. Did he know who she was? DID HE KNOW WHERE I LIVED?

"Are you going to?"

"What?"

"Give back the magazine. Here, let me see it first."

Well, how would that go? Then Mike would have me dead to rights. And I would still require porno. It was a lose/lose.

"Nononono. Let's just go."

So we went.

The bike I generally dumped on the walk up to my house I now took to the garage and camouflaged with junk that was lying around. What if Mike was trawling the neighbourhood for clues? He wasn't going to get me that easily.

I fled to the bedroom I shared with my brother and closed the door. Since it had no lock, I leaned back against it, and pulled the *Penthouse* out of my pants.

It was heavy. Glossy and luxurious. The cover showed a woman from behind. She was wearing what I thought was a bathing suit and was actually a thong. She had a tattoo on her bum. A butterfly.

A whole lot of new things were happening all at once. I'd never seen an actual, real-life woman in anything close to this sort of pose. I had never seen a thong. I did not know what a tattoo was. I'd never really seen a bum that I could remember (as a household, we weren't exactly a hippie commune).

I will spare you the sad details of what I put that magazine through. I was yet too young to have discovered, ahem, self-care, but let us just say that no single issue of any publication has ever suffered such rough treatment at the hands of its reader. There was a lot of rolling around on top of it.

All bound, printed material expands with use. If a book is two inches thick when you pull it off the shelf new, it's three inches by the time you've thumbed all the way through it.

Years later, I'd work at a bookstore through university. People would routinely return books weeks after they'd bought them and say things like, "It was a gift and she already had it." Then they'd hand me the book. Each and every time, it would have expanded to twice the size it had been new. In one case, I'm pretty sure the woman had dropped it in a tub. The book was fanned out like an accordion.

I'd take hold of the book, turn it around in my hands doubtfully and say, "She already had it?"

"Yes. It was a gift."

"For your friend?"

"Yes."

They knew I was going to give them their money back and I knew I was going to give them their money back, but I didn't think it was right that it should be easy. If you want to read a book for free, our social democracy has taken care of that problem for you—it's called a library.

However terribly those cheats treated their literature, it was gentle compared to what I'd done. That *Penthouse* started out a regular-sized magazine. It ended up the thickness of a phone book. I went through that thing front-to-goddamn-back every day for months. I flattened each page out so that I could control the glare on the page, and so see everything clearly all at once.

I would sit in class counting the minutes until I could get back to the magazine and enjoy some quiet reading time. I considered bringing it to school for a lunchtime peek, but that was very risky. I didn't mind the idea that someone else might see it. It was the thought that someone might take it from me.

Most of what was in there made absolutely no sense to me—there was a bunch of swinging lifestyle stuff and a guide to buying a stereo system. But I read it anyway. It wasn't just the pictures—in particular, Butterfly Lady—that obsessed. It all seemed of a piece. In order to be a viable conduit to sexual desire, it required completeness. I assumed there were ideas in there that would only become clear to me later. I needed to be prepared.

A great many books have given me pleasure—in fact, aside from people, nothing has given me so much cumulative joy as books—but the *Penthouse* was the high-water mark. If the amount of time and effort you devote to a piece of literature is the truest expression of its value, that issue of *Penthouse* was my Gutenberg Bible.

Fittingly, this bargain was Faustian.

Since I'd stolen the *Penthouse* from Mike's and been seen doing so, I could no longer go there. The store was on a busy corner. I would time my walk up to the corner so that I could shuffle by quickly on the green light.

It wouldn't have been so bad if I hadn't been expected to go to Mike's at least daily. Every time my mother needed milk, or cigarettes, or anything else really. The sentence I now dreaded most was "Go to Mike's and get _____."

Mike's was two blocks from our house. The next closest convenience store was eight. My mother would hand me money. I'd nod disconsolately and say, "Yes. I'll be right back with _____."

Like most children, I believed my mother was always onto me (unlike most mothers, she was). Of course she would know exactly how long it should take me to get to Mike's and back. And I was convinced she was sitting there at the kitchen table, timing the journey out. Eventually, she was going to say the sentence I dreaded even more: "Why did that take you so long?" Followed by, "What have you done?" Followed by, "Let's ask Mike."

So I'd try to leave the house nonchalantly. Once on the sidewalk, I'd break into a sprint. I could get to the other store pretty quickly. But then there was always a lineup, or some old codger who wanted to have a conversation with the clerk. Seconds counted. I became the world's brusquest seven-year-old: "Excuse me, I'm in a hurry. Can I just get in there? Yes, thank you. Sorry. Thank you."

Occasionally loaded down with groceries, I'd try to haul ass back.

Nothing disturbs people more than seeing someone running who is quite obviously not out for a jog. It begs the question, "What are they running from?" It is doubly disturbing when the person running is a child schlepping bags and panting like an animal. Adults would occasionally get right in my way and stop me.

"Are you all right?"

The first few times this happened, I tried to explain. I was out getting groceries for my mother and in a bit of a rush. But I suppose I did not present a convincing figure—red-faced, bug-eyed, hair all over the place. I probably looked like I'd just crawled out of a sex dungeon.

These little interruptions had a way of stretching on as the grown-up tried to convince him/herself that this was all on the up-and-up and they weren't going to see my picture in the paper the next day.

Eventually, I learned to recognize the signs of concern. The way a person up ahead would stop and begin registering the oddness of what was approaching. The subtle shift of the hips as they began to angle themselves to intercept me.

So in time, I began treating them like tackling dummies. I'd begin to feint one way. As they moved in that direction, I'd juke the other way. Then I'd blow past them. Invariably, they were left, fingers raised in the universal "Excuse me" gesture.

When I got home, I'd be in a bit of a state. The smart thing would have been to take a minute to gather myself on the porch. But time was my only worry. I'd burst through the door, sucking air, and throw the bags down, resisting the powerful desire to lie down on the floor.

My mother was one of those people who always seemed to be coming around a corner, like she'd been waiting for you to arrive the whole time.

"What's the matter with you?"

"Nothing. I ran."

"Why'd you run?"

"No reason."

"Are you *sweating*?"

"A little maybe."

"Running that far shouldn't be so hard for someone your age."

"Maybe."

Over the years, my mother and I shared many conversations that hinged entirely on the word "Maybe." A good word that, crucially, is neither a confirmation nor a denial.

This track-and-field farce went on for months. Mike loomed large in my imagination. What if I saw him on the street? What if he saw me coming out of my house? Every time the doorbell rang, my first thought was, "He's here." I knew that the best way to protect myself was to get rid of the *Penthouse*. Destroy the evidence. But I could not be parted from it. Flipping through it each night had become a profound ritual.

Then one Sunday, on the way home from church, my mother announced that my brother and I would be getting treats. At Mike's.

There was no scene at the door. I didn't hesitate on the street. She didn't have to drag me into the store. I just gave in. My suffering was near its end. I'd just take whatever I had coming.

I tried to shamble in sideways, hiding my face from view. I moved around the store in a sort of crouch. My brother was making a lot of goddamned noise and attracting a lot of attention. I shushed him and he punched me. More attention.

As we got to the counter, I tried to retract my head into my shirt. There was no one behind the counter. We waited a bit. It was excruciating.

Then Mike appeared from the back.

Except it wasn't Mike. It was some other guy. A white guy.

Relief. It isn't a good feeling. It's the sudden, delightful absence of bad feeling, which is far better. Your vision of the world brightens in that moment. The greater the relief, the longer its effect. I would coast on this hit of relief for weeks.

Mike's, I would later learn, had been sold. This was the new owner. The key burden of my life had just burned off like mist. I had got away with my crime.

I think I learned a lesson that day. I'm fairly sure it was the wrong one.

MY BEDROOM

THE FIRST THING I REMEMBER READING out loud was *The Cat in the Hat*. This was in a kindergarten run by nuns. I often carried a book around as a prop and must've picked it up osmotically. The nuns were delighted. I was delighted. My mother was delighted. Everyone was delighted.

One of the Felician Sisters propped me up on her knee and invited me to read to the rest of them at dinner. They clapped when I finished a page. It's just about my earliest memory.

That was also my first experience of positive feedback from the people at work, and I liked it.

But reading was not high on my list for a long time. Not unless it was comic books or my single dirty magazine. I was only interested in literature that did not have the stink of school.

Once people see you with a book, that's what you'll be getting for every birthday and Christmas for the rest of your life. Books are cheap, simple and good for you. Like steel-cut oats or calisthenics. The effect works both ways. Gifting a book leaves a residue of virtue on the giver. I was awash in books that I had no intention of reading. The shelves in the room I shared with my brother were full of them.

What I really needed was space of my own.

If you are cut a certain way, most of your childhood is spent in search of a corner of the world you can have to yourself. When I was young, children were never alone at home. We'd eat with other people, watch TV with them, sleep with them. The only time we had to ourselves was in the bathroom, which is why mothers were always yelling at us through the door to get out of there. The assumption is that a child on his own is in the process of killing himself by accident.

In order for us to be alone, we had to go outside. Where it was often cold or hot, and occasionally rained. You know who spends most of their time outside? Hobos. That's what children used to be—unwilling vagrants.

Some friends and I constructed a fort in the midst of a thicket on the grounds of a palliative-care hospital a few blocks from our house. "Constructed" is a bit ambitious. We'd wedged ourselves in there one day, found a hollow at the centre of a large bush and dug the floor down a foot. It was cramped and filthy. You couldn't stand up. With three of us in there, there was nothing to do but sit cross-legged in a tight circle staring at each other.

But we went there often. After a while, we stopped going together. It became a sort of *pied-à-terre* for the grade-school set north of St. Johns Road. It was a place to unwind. Read *Spider-Man*. Have a nap. Through gaps in the foliage, watch patients being pushed around the lawn in wheelchairs.

If another friend was in there when you arrived, he'd leave. We understood that none of us had any personal space at home and it was rude to bogart the fort all to yourself. Solitude was something we could share evenly.

We lived in a tight, two-bedroom bungalow. My brother and I shared quarters in a room so small you had to climb over one bed to get to the other. I tried to institute the same sharing economy that operated at the fort. At certain times, he could be in the room alone, and at others it would just be me. He wouldn't go for that.

That room became an occupied space, with a thin DMZ down the middle. Most of our fights had to do with something of his touching something of mine. He thought it was unfair that in order to enter and exit the room I had to cross over his territory. My mother suggested we tape a border onto the floor of the room, with an understanding that all crossings of the frontier would be negotiated beforehand. That led to further civil unrest and a deeper retrenching of our positions. Peace talks ended in punch-ups. Neither of us would leave the bedroom, not even to watch television in the living room. It was principled masochism.

The only time my brother was not in that room was on Saturday mornings. He had some class or lesson or swimming or I don't know what it was to go to. That was my special time. I'd close the door and rearrange my stuff. I couldn't just lie there. My mother had a deep aversion to sloth. She hated naps and would not allow one to take place in her presence. Woe to you if she got home at 6 p.m. and found you dozing on the couch. There would be consequences.

She had a theory that no one could sleep if both their feet were planted on the ground. She would leave you like that in the morning—half-in, half-out, in a tortured yoga pose—lest you drift off and miss the bell. We learned to sleep with our legs hanging off the side of a bed, soles squarely on the ground. Eventually, I could do it for hours. It was a hard-won skill that has not repaid the effort it took to learn.

My mother would sometimes say, "If you want to sleep, you can do it in the yard."

She caught me out there once, spread-eagled and face down in the grass. After that, the yard was no longer available as a sleeping option.

Buried deep in our lizard brain, each of us has a phrase we remember our mothers saying that caused instant panic. If you think of it now, it still has that power. In my case, it was, "Are you sleeping in there?"

There was also the way she said my name in the morning when she was losing her temper because I wasn't yet up. She had a particular way of emphasizing the first syllable—"CA-thal? CA-thal?? CA-thal??!"—that allowed me to gauge just how bad it was getting.

My name wasn't her idea. It was my father's. He was less "Irish" than my mother, in the sense that his family moved to Canada when he was nine years old. He didn't have the accent. He couldn't speak the Irish language. My mother arrived in her mid-twenties and had both of those advantages. My father was always trying to close the authenticity gap that separated them. He made a big show of listening to Irish music and going to Irish events and hanging around at the Irish Centre. Giving me a weird, non-phonetic, unpronounceable name was part of his effort at ethnic advertising. My mother let him have the first kid. When he tried slapping the name Pádraig on my brother, she revolted.

I hated my name as a child because it often made me the excruciating centre of attention. Teachers were especially poor at understanding that the way to figure out how to say a kid's name is by taking him/her to the side and asking, not standing up in front of the class and turning it around in their mouths like they were being asked to speak Klingon.

When I changed high schools, the teacher in my first class asked me to get up and tell everyone what it was like to live in Ireland. I told him I was Canadian. He began to argue with me about it.

"But you told me you were from Ireland."

I had done no such thing. He'd asked where my name was from, and I said, "It's Irish."

"Why would you tell me that if it's not true?"

"I didn't."

"Yes, you did. You told me that."

Oh, for the love of God.

When I think of my name now, it creates a thought chain— the word, the way my mother said the word, trying to sleep as she said the word, lying in bed, knowing I could not be asleep, reading.

Reading was the way I walled in my Saturday morning castle. My mother couldn't argue with that. What was she going to say—"Stop being so lazy. Go into the living room and watch TV"? I didn't read because I liked reading. I read because I wanted to be left alone.

Someone had given me a Hardy Boys novel that looked short and simple. One day, I took it into bed and lay there with it. In the movie of my life, a string section would launch as I opened to the first page. Those books were as much a formula as the

Second Law of Thermodynamics. They were always the same. Every plot had the same twists, in the same order, on the same beats.

These kids had cracked, like, two dozen jewellery heists and a couple of murders, and yet in the middle of every second act, no one in town would believe they were telling the truth.

"The body's hidden in the old copper mineshaft. I saw Mr. Jenkins put it there."

"I don't know, Frank. Sounds pretty crazy to me. Do you have any proof?"

"Well, there are those hundreds of career criminals Joe and I put into prison in our spare time between 4-H and football practice. We stand on our record as the most successful and prolific detectives in human history."

"I see your point, but still . . ."

That was what I liked about the Hardy Boys—you knew exactly what you were getting. There was a comfort in that.

The allowance that had once gone entirely to comics was being diverted to the Hardy Boys. I bought a new one each week. There are a kajillion of them and I could read an entire adventure in a single morning. Start it around eight, get to the end around noon.

That's something you could be proud of. You'd *finished* a book. You could devote a whole lifetime to getting through the Hardy Boys canon and, like raking a Zen garden, it would not be a wasted life.

All of us hope that at some early point in our lives, we will find the thing we are meant to do. Paleontology or paddle boarding or nuclear physics. In the best-case scenario, it's something we can eventually do for a living. At the least, it should be something you aren't ashamed to tell people about at parties—"Serial killing, that's my passion. I work as a clown on the weekends, and that's great. The kids and all. But serial killing's where my heart's at."

Many people will be disappointed on this score. They can do all sorts of things, have jobs and friends, are fully functional, but they don't have a thing that they are driven to do.

I was lucky. I found my thing early. It's reading in bed. Not just reading, but reading in bed. Admittedly, it's just barely an activity. If you called it slothful, I would find it hard to argue. But I have spent more time doing that than anything else. It gives me an abiding pleasure that has never flagged.

Long before I went out into the world, books had given me some idea of how it worked. I consumed them. I've read thousands. They introduced me to a cross-section of human experience. They gave me the foundation upon which to construct an identity. If you read widely and with an open heart, you have been tutored by the most searching minds in human history—either the writers themselves or the people they are writing about.

You will never know everything about how this all works and what it all means, but if you read, you can get close.

A room of my own, a bed and a book. That's all I need now and all I craved as a child.

The land squabble with my brother was solved, Solomon-like, when my mother bought us a bunkbed. By the ancient and immutable rights of first-born, I should have got the top bunk. But my brother wheedled it out of her.

It was a pyrrhic victory. Now if he wanted to be in the room, he had to be constantly climbing up and down a ladder. He abandoned his perch soon after and it feels as if I never really saw him again. I was always in the bedroom, and he was always somewhere else.

I had a little spotlight in there and would spend half the nights reading. I remember being tucked into that burrow with Stephen King's *The Shining* and scaring myself so badly that I had to take the book and put it another room.

My memory for timelines and events has always been poor, but if you hand me a book, I can recall where I was when I read it, what I was doing, how things were going and how I felt. Books and the rooms I read them in are the key signposts of my life. They have been my profoundest consolation.

Years ago, I went to see the Italian author Umberto Eco in conversation. He told a story about his library, which contained ten thousand volumes. Someone had visited his house and marvelled at the number of books. They asked if he'd read all of them, the implication being that someone who'd done that was a person of immense accomplishment. To the visitor, the library was a trophy, the visible evidence of learning.

"Of course I haven't read them all," Eco said he'd told the man. "If I had, why would I keep them?"

That line hit me like a lightning bolt. That was the purpose of life.

Not accumulating knowledge, or rounding out an area of expertise or building a collection.

But recognizing that for some people who come to it early and without being forced, life is a long search for the next great book.

THE LORD OF THE RINGS

NO ONE IN MY FAMILY WAS INTERESTING, at least not in any showy way. They hadn't been anywhere or done anything notable. They were carpenters, miners, tellers and construction workers. They didn't vacation overseas or go to the theatre. Beyond the occasional alcoholic, they had no compulsions or intense interests. Though now in the city, they all tended toward the melancholic rhythm of rural life.

"Did you hear that your man Michael lost his job?"

"Did he now?"

"Sure, he did."

"And what happened there?"

"Couldn't say. Bad luck, I suppose."

"Well, God bless him. I'm sure he'll set himself right soon enough."

There was a lot of that in the kitchen of a Sunday night. It wasn't exactly the Algonquin Table.

We were—and I say this with no small amount of little-guy pride—peasants. My family was one generation removed from serfdom. We've come a ways, but it's still going to take a few iterations to find even a little hint of cosmopolitanism.

There was one person in my extended family who had an adventurous spirit—my mother's elder sister, Sheila. Sheila was the only one of my mother's or father's siblings who didn't emigrate from Ireland (its own sort of adventure, I suppose, but one taken with more fear than joy). That alone made her exotic to me. The one who wouldn't give in. The one who stayed.

Like all the sisters, Sheila was small and wiry. She had a way of looking through you and saying things she oughtn't. She treated children as she did adults—with scorn. Most people disappointed her in their aimlessness and lack of conviction.

She'd had a good job as a civil servant in Dublin, but left it to follow her passion—alternative medicine. She was a hippie without the clothes or calm. She ate macrobiotically—as best I could tell, this meant nothing but a wretched brown rice stew that seemed to be constantly cooking. It smelled awful and would stink up the house for days.

You will never again be as politically open as you are in that gestational period between learning to read and having to first pay taxes, but even I thought Sheila was a bit out there. There was a lot of ranting about the state of the world and retreating to the country for meditation. (It has always struck me that the people who are most enthusiastic about meditation feel the need to constantly *talk* about it, which is rather contrary to the point.)

On one occasion, Sheila offered to demonstrate a massage technique she'd picked up somewhere. This involved badgering me to get down on the floor of our kitchen while she walked on my back. She didn't weigh much more than a child, but I could feel my ribs cracking with each step.

This did not dissuade her in the least as the pain was meant to release tension. The situation devolved from there. She clutched my back like a deranged chimpanzee as I rolled around screaming for mercy. It is one of the very few times I can remember my mother really laughing. She rocked back and forth so hard that she slipped off her chair, crying at the sight of it.

When I started to shriek, "GET HER OFF OF ME!" my mother laughed harder.

From then on, I made sure to keep Sheila in front of me at all times.

Sheila had remained in Ireland to take care of her own mother. By all accounts, my grandmother was a handful. Well into her thirties, she'd been given to my grandfather (neither of them particularly willing) in an arranged marriage so that the farm her family owned could be passed on.

It wasn't a good match. My grandfather had wanted to be a teacher. Now he was a farmer, and not much good at it. In large part, he rented the land out to people better suited to make money from it.

My mother's parents had five children—the first, a daughter, died young of disease—and lived together in a wary truce. She was very much the boss of him and he spent a lot of time out in the fields pretending to work but actually just hiding from his wife. My mother likes to tell a story about her mother finding her father tucked up against a stone wall, reading when he was supposed to be tilling, and beating him with a broom for his laziness.

My mother took me to meet her once. She wasn't impressed by me. She sat there on the stool by the fireplace in a long, formless black smock, like a priest's habit, legs splayed, hands propped on knees, regarding me without much interest. When my mother tried to push me toward her, I backed away instinctively and nearly into the fire. My sweater briefly lit up.

"Not too clever, is he?" my grandmother said.

I spent the rest of that visit out in the front yard chasing chickens. There was another boy about my age living down the road (it was a two-house town). His name was Bob. His only hobby was taking a bicycle up to the top of the hill that led down to his family's stucco cottage, riding it as fast as he could down the slope, slamming it into the front wall of his house, meticulously repairing the damage and starting the process over again.

Country life. It's not for me.

My grandmother had been particularly hard on Sheila, and in the unfair way of things, it was Sheila who ended up taking care of her as she lay dying. When she passed and it came time to divide up the meagre possessions, Sheila was jobbed out of her inheritance. This set the entire family to fighting. Eventually, the home place was sold to an American hobbyist looking to get back to his roots. The cottage was levelled. How long had it been there? A hundred years? More? Nothing ever stays the same.

She'd whip over to Canada from time to time to preach at us at the highest possible volume. She had her opinions and was one of those people who assumed at the outset that you disagreed with them. Whether you did or not was immaterial. What Sheila wanted was the opportunity to hector you about her ideas. She was forever talking.

We had a great many enjoyable interactions that involved her jabbing a finger at me while I stood there woodenly having no idea what she was on about. Genetically engineered crops or the evils of the medical–industrial complex. She would've made a wonderful cadre during the Cultural Revolution. This was someone who could see you burned for your sins and feel forever that it was the right thing to do.

After quitting the good government job, she took work as a maid in Boston, where she studied something in the field we might now call "wellness." She was my first model of a person living exactly as they wanted to—which is perhaps why I am leery of the concept. I'd eventually decide it's better to throw yourself in life's river and let the current take you where it will, with minor course corrections achieved through panicked flailing.

She was the closest we ever came in my family to a Marlon Brando figure—someone stitched together from their passions. Someone uncivil and magnetic.

The one tangible thing I have remaining of Sheila is a book.

On one of her swannings through town, she gave me a single bound copy of the *Lord of the Rings* trilogy. I may have been nine or ten at the time. I'd never owned a volume that was so *heavy*. That was what struck me first. The thing was huge—1,077 pages of tight script on rice paper. It was my first experience of being daunted by literature.

I asked what it was about.

"Just read it," Sheila said.

"But you know, is it about . . ."

"Just read it"—more annoyed this time.

This was grade four or so. People—teachers, librarians—were forever telling me which books I couldn't read. They weren't trying to protect me from the content. Rather, they assumed that my mind worked on one level and that most books were on another, higher than that. A librarian at our school once snuck up on me from behind, pulled a book out of my hand and said, "You won't like that."

How would she know? Had she read it? Was it not good? "That's for later."

So of course I wanted these forbidden books. I spent most of my allowance on comics because I had no access to a bookstore. I'm sure there was one in our neighbourhood, but no one took me there. I got my books at the library, through the age-appropriate gatekeepers.

Sheila was the first person who had given me an "adult" book.

At first, I didn't need to read *The Lord of the Rings*. Possessing it was enough. I liked to hold it and shuffle the pages back and forth. I'd land somewhere in the middle and hope that someone would walk into my bedroom at that moment. They'd catch me at it and think, "What a fascinating person he must be, reading such a large book."

I did eventually try to read it, but that book thwarted me. *The Lord of the Rings* is one of those beloved novels—*Moby Dick* is probably the *ne plus ultra*—that is overwritten to the point of occasional incomprehensibility. (Melville's opus was rejected by dozens of publishers before its eventual success. One of the refuseniks replied, "First, we must ask, does it have to be a whale?" and "Could not the captain be struggling with a depravity towards young, perhaps voluptuous, maidens?" We laugh at the poor guy now, but he had a point.)

A certain sort of classic enters the canon because the few people who've done the hard work of getting through it very badly need other people to know what they've accomplished. Otherwise, why have bothered to learn about the minutiae of ambergris?

Every few weeks, I'd get thirty or forty pages into *The Lord of the Rings*—understanding very little of what was going on, a

birthday party or somesuch that never seems to actually start—
and give up. I'd put it away for a while. Then I'd spot it on the
shelf during a quiet moment and decide to try again. I suppose
I continued trying because I didn't want to come up short in
Sheila's eyes. She'd thought me bright enough to tackle this
thing, and I would. Whether I enjoyed doing so or not.

Years passed. At least two. Maybe three.

On one unremarkable Saturday, it finally clicked. I picked
the book up again, began reading and did not stop. The story
had managed to get hold of me. Reading remains the one thing
we can do compulsively and feel no guilt about. This was my
first experience of that.

Once you are grown, you read differently. Now you're
hoovering up information. You're piling a few things you didn't
yet know onto all the things you already do. You may read
better, make better connections and comparisons, but you no
longer read deeply. You're walking on territory that's already
been mapped, adding more points of orientation.

I read that book like it was the first book I'd ever encountered. It was—and maybe this word is too much and isn't meant
in the literal sense—magical.

I assume most people are familiar with the story—hobbits,
a ring, dark lord, good wizards, bad wizards, a journey, trolls,
near-death experiences, a volcano.

It wasn't the story that got to me. It was its detail. Someone
had spent years constructing an edifice of imagination that lacked
in no particulars. He'd thought about the language and the flowers and the way things felt to the touch. He wasn't pulling you
through it. He was planting you in the middle of it and pointing
out every single thing. Tolkien taught me that we are not trapped

in this world. We can construct our own. You felt his guiding hand in it.

There are many authors I think I know better as friends than most real people I've encountered. He was the first.

At twelve years old, it was still hard sledding. The ornateness of the vocabulary defeated me. The metaphors and allusions were so far out of my experience, they did not reach me. But the intimacy of description enthralled me, it all felt urgent and personal. It was a very long message in a bottle—"Here's everything that happened."

Like all the art that has hit me hardest, the narrative was about outcasts and loners finding each other. Despite the creature-y aspect, it's a love story and a tale of redemption. The good guys win, but they suffer in the effort. That's what Tolkien was saying. That reached me.

For many of the days that followed, whenever I was away from it, I pined to have that book back in my hands. I thought about it in the classroom and the schoolyard. I didn't dare bring it anywhere for fear of losing it. After all, it had come from Europe.

More than the story, I remember the way the book felt, the way it sagged in my hand under its own weight, the dull crack it made as the bulk of its pages adjusted in turning.

As I neared the end, I slowed. I didn't want this feeling to stop. What if I never found another book like this? What if Sheila had given me *the best book*, and I'd already hit the peak of my reading life? What could follow this? When we are children, every experience is whole and complete, unconnected to any other. Every day, every book, every trip, every encounter might be an odyssey, something completely unlike anything we've felt before.

Think of how you felt when you were a kid and someone said, "Tomorrow, we are going to the store."

The store! What might happen there? What would you see? Maybe you'd come back with something incredible you hadn't known existed until you found it there. At the store.

Now it's, "Christ, remind me to go to the store."

For a while, everything is new. And then it isn't. You realize all things are connected, and nothing is unlike any other. It's the coping mechanism that makes life bearable as well as dull.

I read that book over and over again. I read it ragged trying to rediscover in it the same feeling I'd had when I encountered it the first time. Each pass through grew shorter and less sweet. After a while, it began to fall apart. The binding has come completely undone. It's become a loose collection of pages held together by scotch tape. When I wanted to reread *The Lord of the Rings*, I bought a few cheap, beater copies for the purpose. Sheila's gift had become the classic car of my collection—too precious to drive.

They made movies from it. That ruined everything. Now every muppet who hadn't taken the time and effort to get this thing from the source could have a bowdlerized copy of it, a visual Coles Notes. Nine hours, start to finish. I watched them and have never since felt the desire to reread the book. They made my particular experience of it common.

But if the house was to catch fire and I could only save a few things, that book would be one of them. It's the one book I own that I take off the shelf every now and again, just to hold and flip through it.

There is no inscription. We weren't sentimental that way.

HOCKEY

WE OFTEN DISCUSS SPORTS AS A WAY OUT—of whatever life we're living, of our worries. In Canada, hockey is a way in. Playing it or following it pushes you into the mainstream. It was once the key to belonging.

My mother immigrated to Canada from Ireland in 1970. She came with her sister. Other than that, she didn't know anyone. She quickly found office work, embedded herself in the local Irish community and hooked up with my father.

Her first touchstone in the country was the Hamill family—they were also working-class Irish immigrants, but more settled and attuned to Canada's rhythms. My mother and her sister briefly lived with them upon arrival. The patriarch of that family, Mickey, was a very particular Irish sort—loud, jolly and just a bit vicious. He worked construction and excelled at Gaelic sports—hurling and football. Unfortunately, Mickey had been banned for life from the local clubs after cracking a hurling stick over the head of a referee while arguing a call. He continued to insist it was a reasonable thing to do. I can see his point.

When you give a man a stick and agree that he may use it in violence, he's going to do so. Occasionally, he's going to do so contrary to the rules you imposed upon him.

We would often spend Saturday evenings jammed into the Hamills' tiny front room. The adults sat around drinking and smoking (I remember that room as so thick with cigarette smoke that it was as hazy as a sauna). I would watch them drink or smoke, trying to figure out what made a joke a joke and why people would laugh at certain arrangements of words and not others.

They would talk. Mickey would not. That drew me to watching Mickey.

While the others jabbered, Mickey perched on the edge of the couch watching *Hockey Night in Canada* on a television perhaps two feet from his face. Like all seventies TV sets, the Hamills' was more furniture than appliance—a wooden cabinet the size of a refrigerator turned on its side.

Looking back on it, I'm not sure Mickey understood the finer points of hockey. He would shriek mantras that had very little to do with the nuances of the game: "OUT! OUT! OUUUUUUTTT!" or "GO! GO YE FECKIN' EEJIT! GOOOO!"

What made an impression on me was the passion.

If anyone happened to walk in front of the television set, Mickey would set to frantically waving his arms over his head like a presenting orangutan. He couldn't bring himself to yell at his friends, but he also couldn't bear to miss a moment of whatever the Toronto Maple Leafs were doing (usually quite poorly).

As he watched, Mickey would gradually bend forward until he was in a low crouch, knees practically on the ground, hands raised slightly in a gesture of grasping. His bum would begin to slide off the seat. His eyes were bugged out. He looked perpetually in the motion of tackling.

When it came time for a commercial break, Mickey would swing back suddenly to the vertical, as if regaining consciousness. He'd be red-faced, clammy and a bit breathless. He'd press his hair back and cheerily engage whoever was sitting alongside him (the worst seat in the room) for precisely two minutes. Then he would break off conversation just as suddenly and recommence screaming at the television.

I'd stand in a corner observing his gestures—the hands, the yelling, the simian flailing. I would occasionally catch my mother watching me watching Mickey. She'd make a shooing gesture. I'd move into one of her blind spots for a minute or two, and then return to my observations.

I have always been very aware of people watching me. (Though no one ever really is. There is no greater misapprehension in life than the belief that others are as fascinated by you as you are by yourself.) Mickey did not have this sickness. He didn't care how he appeared to others. He was a man entirely comfortable with himself. It's a rare gift.

Eventually, my fascination with Mickey began to extend to his fixation. What was it about hockey that made Mickey kneel down in front of the television, grip the cabinet so hard it was in danger of splintering, and then scream, "NO! NO! NO!"?

It was around this time that my mother insisted I begin playing hockey. She had a five-skill plan that I suppose was meant to turn me into a contributing citizen who could pass for Canadian. I was expected to learn five things—how to skate, how to swim, how to ride a bike, how to drive and how to touch-type. That she was right about the value of all five didn't make it any less irritating.

I eventually became reasonably proficient at four of them, but skating didn't take.

I played hockey for years, somehow getting worse at it as I went along. Despite hours of "power skating" lessons—the Canadian iteration of a fad diet—I never did learn how to stop with a leading left foot. Or skate backward. Or move from side to side.

As tends to happen with the weaklings at the beginner level, my first coach made me a defenceman. Since I skated backward so poorly, my only option was to grab hold of opponents and pull them to the ice as they went by me. When it became clear that that sort of thing was punished but also tolerated, my criminal hockey behaviour worsened. I was out there on the ice like an out-of-control top, wheeling around wildly in search of a solid object to fell. It was Newtonian physics without any of the grace.

At the height of this flagrant disregard for the norms of the game, I grabbed hold of the puck in my own goalie's crease and rather than shovel it out shoved it down my pants instead. Why? Well, why not? Once you do something so stupid, you have to stand tall. Not by admitting it, but by deepening the lie. Several people had seen me steal the puck, including the referee, but I insisted they were wrong.

No adult man was going to jam his hands down the front of a seven-year-old's pants. I was removed to a dressing room and instructed to strip. I refused. Several adults were brought in to press me. I rebuffed each one. Eventually, they found another puck and the game resumed. I was ejected and walked home in my hockey uniform, minus skates.

I spent years slapping that puck against a garage door—a pointless way to spend your spare time and a good way to ruin a door—but having claimed the thing through nefarious means, I enjoyed getting some use out of it.

When my mother heard the story, she agreed that keeping the puck was the proper thing to do.

"Sure, what do they need a puck for anyway?" she said. "They must have dozens of the things."

My mother and I rarely agreed on much, but she did love assuming my proxy in any tussle with authority. Never submit, especially when you're in the wrong. That was my mother's credo.

The puck incident did blight my nascent hockey career, which didn't bother me in the least.

For some reason, Canada has arranged youth hockey on an insomniac's schedule—no game can start after 8 a.m. Which means you have to be up at 6. During winter. When it's cold and dark. For generations of Canadian children, hockey is like working in a coal mine, on your days off.

What I did like about hockey was the brutality. The ice was a place of consequence-free violence in which we could not do each other any real harm—all of us being too light and too well armoured. As long as you didn't hit anyone with your stick (the Mickey Hamill Rule), just about everything fell under the banner of "working off some steam." I worked off a lot of steam.

It was the actual play that escaped me since balance and suppleness have never been my strong suits. At one point, I very badly wanted to be a skateboarder. The first time I got on a friend's board, I managed to tentatively put both feet up on the deck. Then I made the mistake of swinging one leg out for an almighty push-off. The board flew out from underneath me, sending me sprawling backward. I landed like an anvil on the concrete and was knocked unconscious.

When I came to, none of my friends had moved from the spots they were in when I'd fallen. I don't think it was that they didn't care. It was that they didn't want to further embarrass me by helping. A half-dozen of them stood there in funereal silence while I lay on the ground deciding if I wanted to vomit now or vomit when I got home.

From then on, I concentrated on the lifestyle aspects of skateboarding—largely the music—rather than actual skate-boarding. It was a sensible compromise.

Much the same rule applied in hockey. I would agree not to play it, but I would try to enjoy it nonetheless.

My father also watched hockey, but morosely. For him, the sport was a national duty. He'd sit by himself with a drink in his hand boring his eyes dully into the screen. Occasionally, he'd let off a "Terrible," or a "Jesus CHRIST." He didn't make it look like much fun. He was a Maple Leafs fan in the way most Torontonians were Maple Leafs fans in the 1970s—unwillingly.

His family had moved to North Bay, Ontario, from Ireland when he was young, so I knew he could play, but had never seen it. The only time he talked about hockey was with his brothers, when they'd argue who'd been best. They told a story about my uncle Finnan having been given a tryout for the Leafs, but I very much doubted it. It is a habit of Irish families (and maybe other families as well—I couldn't say) to have often been close enough to greatness to have brushed past it, but never in any objectively provable way. This is why my mother's side con-tinues to insist we are distantly related to James Joyce. They are impervious to the argument that, on an island with a population of four million, everyone is a distant relation of everyone else.

My single hockey memory of my father is going with him to Toronto's High Park for a leisure skate on a public rink. It was late afternoon on a Saturday. We didn't often go out on my weekends with him, so this excursion was already remarkable. He got roped into a game of shinny with some twenty-year-olds. Someone gave him a stick and lent him gloves. He'd probably been drinking, but he was still fully functional.

I watched from the bench. For ten minutes, he enjoyed himself. That thought occurred to me: "He's having fun." I don't think I'd ever before seen that. He was also more than a little good. He was one of the best out there. Even the younger men, many of them decent players, were obviously impressed. I felt myself expanding.

One of the rules of shinny is that you don't raise the puck, since no one is wearing pads. Eventually, someone always raises the puck. One nitwit took a hard slapshot into a crowd that nailed my dad in the chest. The game stopped. Only I knew what was coming.

My father went down on one knee, clutching at himself. The other players gathered around. A few of them looked stricken— they'd just taken out the old fella. My father would have been in his mid-thirties at the time, still formidable. He was of average height, but thick. He'd done hard labour in his youth and that strength never really leaves you.

Someone helped my father up. After a few minutes' recovery, he asked who'd taken the shot. The dummy stepped forward for ritual absolution. He was young-ish, but not young. Maybe he was there with his kid as well.

He had his hand extended in a gesture of conciliation when my father punched him in the face. It was a square blow, which is not easy to do. He buckled. My father dropped on top of him and began swinging. There was now a pile of men on the ice, most of them trying to help but not doing a good job of it. Accidental elbows spread the rage around, turning peacemakers into combatants. For a moment, it was a proper brawl.

But fist fighting is hard work. Amateurs tire quickly. In short order, it was just a bunch of exhausted people lying on top of each other in the middle of the ice.

They pulled my father up. He wasn't a big man, but he lacked fear. He was still very much up for it. What I recall most was that he didn't say anything. Everyone else had resumed shouting. The guy who'd been punched was being ushered away by his own friends, jabbing out a finger and yelling threats. A few of them tugged at him without conviction, saying things like, "Forget it."

My father was taken back to the boards without an angry word. Though he strained at the arms of the people holding him, his face was impassive. You wouldn't know he was angry to look at him. That was his trick.

I also suspected that if the other guy's friends had let him go, he would most likely have stood there continuing to threaten. And if they'd let go of my father, he would've gone back in with a stick until one of them was dead.

I went over to take a hold of his arm. Once the rest of them saw him with a little kid, the emotional temperature dropped. The situation suddenly seemed quite sad. My father said something about the borrowed gloves and someone else said not to worry, they'd find them. He looked back at his opponent with more hurt than rage. He walked awkwardly to a bench to take off his skates. I tried to help steady him, but he shrugged me off.

"What did you think?" he said to me. He was bent over, working at his laces. He hadn't looked at me yet. I wasn't sure what part of it he meant—the hockey or the fight—so I opted for brightness.

"It was really good."

That was the only time I ever saw him play.

We continued to watch hockey together, usually in total silence. He wasn't interested in my thoughts on the matter (he'd seen me play). I suppose he thought it was something a father should do with a son and, unlike most other activities, this one put him in proximity to the liquor cabinet. It was a reasonable compromise.

There are two types of father–son sports relationships—one in which son adopts father's team and the pair of them grow closer together through a shared obsession; and the kind my dad and I had.

At that time, the Leafs were a flaming wreck of a team whose only purpose seemed to be embarrassing the city. There was one player my father admired above all others—Börje Salming.

Whereas most of the Leafs looked like baboons who'd had skates stapled to the soles of their feet, Salming was a silky craftsman. In close-ups during breaks in play, he often looked pained to be sharing the ice with this gaggle of louts and nit-wits. I liked that about him—the man who could do better for himself but chose to suffer nonetheless.

I assumed it had something to do with being Swedish, that they must be better than us. After visiting Stockholm, I've decided I was right.

One day, Salming showed up at my baseball game, causing pandemonium amongst the rubes of the High Park Little League.

Few things stick with you more than your first brush with celebrity. Just last night, this person was on your television, no more real to you than Wile E. Coyote. And now here he is, in life. Your life. Breathing the same air and being in the same space. It's disorienting and wonderful.

He was bigger than I'd expected and remarkably fit. His arms were ropey and his hands wide as shovels. I'd never seen so *manly* a man. I felt a powerful need to touch him.

He signed a hat for me and gave me the sort of serious nod men give to other men but not children. I would've preferred that he'd said something, but maybe this was what respect looked like. My father didn't come to my games, and there was a wicked joy in knowing he'd missed this.

Salming was there because he'd just enrolled his son on our team. I don't remember that kid's name. I do remember two things about him—that, even at that age, he was preposterously handsome—white-blond hair, limpid blue eyes, a precursor to a Gap Kids print ad—and that he was a truly awful baseball player. Salming's kid played so poorly, you began to wonder if the local mafia had taken an interest in point shaving little league games.

We played once a week. Salming came every time. He arrived alone, always wearing a t-shirt and a fleece vest (he was the first person I'd ever seen wear one and that also seemed exotic). He'd take a seat at the edge of the small bleachers so that the constant stream of people approaching him for autographs wouldn't disturb the other parents. He was Buddha-esque in his stillness.

Salming never spoke that I saw. People would try to engage him in conversation and he'd nod at them benevolently until they stopped. He didn't yell encouragement at the players like everyone else or clap when his own kid came to bat. He just watched.

Eventually, I started to resent that. Why wasn't he being more helpful? Why wasn't he taking his kid—who couldn't catch a beachball if he'd had flypaper glued to his palms—out in the backyard to practise? And why hadn't he telepathically figured out how much I wanted him to talk to me?

His whole mien seemed selfish. He'd done okay in sports life, but now his son was being left out there to dangle. People assumed Salming's kid would be as good at baseball as his father was at hockey, and it wasn't working out. Nobody judged him out loud, but we were all thinking it. Wasn't Salming ashamed? Didn't he care? Why wouldn't he come over after the game like the other fathers and high-five the players? Did he think he was better than us?

After a short while, Salming's son left the team and Salming stopped coming. I held that against him, too. There had been a lot of reflected glory from playing on the same team as Börje Salming's kid. Now he'd robbed us of that.

I'd been ambivalent about the Leafs, but this general souring on Börje Salming turned into a genuine dislike of the team. Here was the best of them, and he wasn't much use in actual life.

Of course, none of this makes any sense. I suppose Salming, through no fault of his own, became a stand-in for my father, and that in failing to notice me for the special little person I hoped I was, he'd failed me. It's ridiculous, but there it is.

I learned to hate the Leafs because my father liked them, and because his favourite player didn't know I wanted a hug.

So, like many other Toronto-born front runners my age, I became a New York Islanders fan. They were easy to love—far and away the best team in the NHL and very unlikely to be run into at the grocery store or in gym class. Bryan Trottier wasn't going to ruin it by brushing past me after I'd extended my hand for a shake.

I was a Mike Bossy man. My brother, who had very little to do with my father, became a Wayne Gretzky guy in opposition. It was in the midst of explaining to him why 215 points in a season wasn't quite as impressive as it sounded that I first realized that I was totally full of shit. I wouldn't become a newspaper sports columnist for another quarter-century, but that may have been where the instinct was discovered. Twelve years old and loudly arguing the inarguable.

In the end, my brother was proven right and that also chipped away at hockey for me. By then, I'd moved on to baseball. That had the numbers. You could order it in your mind from a distance, on the page. It didn't require in-person involvement. When I watch hockey now, I do it like my father did—severely, muttering to myself.

Decades later, I saw Salming in the tunnel of the Air Canada Centre before a Leafs game. He was there to be honoured for something or other.

He still looked good. But he was different than I remembered— bright, smiley and plainly delighted to be surrounded by people who wanted to talk. Pros get like that once it's over. Though being loved was an annoyance, they miss it.

I could've gone up to him then and had the talk I'd always wanted. It wouldn't have amounted to much. Just a few blandishments, maybe remind him about the Little League days. Share a laugh. He wouldn't remember, but maybe he'd do me the favour of pretending. It'd be cathartic.

But I couldn't do it. It seemed too much like begging. So I watched him for a while and then left it alone.

In the course of my job, I've met a few genuine legends. Pelé once surprised me with a hug and I nearly sobbed. But Salming remains the only athlete whose autograph I have ever asked for. I may still have that ball cap somewhere. I'm not sure where, and I don't think I want to know.

FIGHTS

NO ONE TEACHES YOU how to fight. You don't realize how important that is until you're in the midst of one.

Whatever most of us do know about fighting we've learned from TV. Square up. Fists held in front of the face. Short jabs. Bob and weave.

Starsky and Hutch made it look easy.

It doesn't work like that. Most fights are wrestling matches from the off. The other guy's on top of you. He's moving frantically, clutching at your clothes, trying to get you off your feet. Lacking any feeling for the way this works, you may try throwing a couple of times. You know your punches should be short, controlled snaps.

They aren't. They're long, looping tosses that a blind man could see coming from across the street. You can't connect. If you can, you're hitting a shoulder or the top of a head—more likely to break a bone in your own hand than hurt the other guy. You don't even know how to clench your fists correctly (thumb tucked protectively under your fingers). If you keep punching, your hands are going to be a mess.

You need to keep your feet moving, but you're tired. An hour of jumping jacks cannot exhaust you more completely than sixty seconds of a fist fight. Half a minute in, you can barely stand. At that point, it becomes dirty. If he gets on top of you, it will get very bad.

You know instinctively what you should be doing—going for the eyes or the crotch, sticking a thumb in his mouth and pulling as hard as you can. But some basic revulsion at causing pain—real, ugly pain—stops you.

In nature, even the most vicious animals are unlikely to badly harm their own kind. Most soldiers in war are unwilling to shoot at the enemy. They have to be trained to do so, their internal barriers broken down until their fear response is to kill. It's called operant conditioning. It's not on the grade-school curriculum.

None of these problems can be course-corrected mid-brawl. You're too amped up on adrenaline. Your brain has ceded control to some Neanderthal remnant of your nervous system. You're not thinking. You're also not feeling anything.

You want to run. That'd be the smart thing to do. But your fear of humiliation is stronger than your aversion to pain. So you stay and take your chances. You're waiting for someone to break it up and save you. Not your body, your pride.

The only way you learn any of this is by taking a beating. A good many of them were handed around at my school at recess.

I had one advantage in the schoolyard—I'd been hit before.

My father was not a disciplinarian. He was a reactionary. You did or said something he didn't like, and he'd reach out and slap you. Not a tap or a warning. Full force.

He had an old yellow Ford pickup. It was rusted out. The paint was flaking off. One day, he came out and found me mindlessly picking away at it, peeling off strips. He didn't say anything. He walked up behind me and hit me so hard in the back of the head that I left my feet and slammed into the bumper.

The next day, he tried making it up to me by letting me sit on his lap and turn the steering wheel as he pulled into the driveway. I lost control and mowed down a section of the neighbour's hedge. He threw me off his lap and into the passenger side door. I was about six.

These weren't beatings. They didn't last past a single blow and didn't happen very often. It would depend on his mood and how much he'd had to drink. I wouldn't have said I was afraid of him. Only wary. I tried to keep him happy and in front of me.

Everyone in my family treated him that way—like a beast that's been uncaged and put on a leash. You're not going to stop it from biting. All you can do is try to keep out of its way.

So I knew from experience that you are unlikely to be badly hurt by being hit. That was useful because I found myself getting hit a lot.

One of my frequent daydreams is putting my adult mind in my childhood body and reliving a day of that life. I wouldn't change anything. I'd only observe. Would the other kids notice? Would I be different? Speak strangely? Carry myself in a more confident way? Because clearly I did it wrong at the time. Around that same age—six or seven—it had dawned on me that I was not a leader. I followed. When you follow, you are a victim-in-training.

I became the particular target of one yard bully, Dino. Dino was a cartoonish version of the type—big, galumphing, buck-toothed, stupid. But also feline in the way he could convince you, if only briefly, that you were friends.

He'd sidle up after he'd given you a good trashing in front of a crowd and say he was sorry, smiling slyly to see how you reacted. You'd think it was over. Then the next day, he'd come over and trash you again. Or the day after. Or a week later. I suppose it was the push–pull that excited him.

After a few months of this, I complained at home. Bizarrely, this prompted my father to launch into a long speech about how fighting was wrong and that I should not do it.

"Well, what should I do then?"

He went back to "fighting is wrong." I should tell a teacher. (Whenever I hear someone say this to a child now, I think, "Would you give that same advice to yourself if someone walked up to you at work and punched you in the mouth? Do you believe your colleagues would think more of you if, instead of throwing back, you ran off to tell human resources?")

Dino continued pummelling me. He would often chase me and my buddy David all the way home. My cardio has never been better. Dino understood that fear of violence is much worse than violence itself. That's another thing you have to learn for yourself.

Complaining at school made it worse.

"Did he hit you?"

"Well, not that time. No."

"Did it happen at school?"

"No."

"Then we can't do anything about it."

Soon, you're labelled a whiner and a malingerer and now you're stuck.

My mother and father split up when I was seven. Freed of my father's erratic presence, my mother began a long process of becoming herself again. She had up to that point been so quiet that she was functionally mute. She had never given me any advice, but now she started.

"When someone hits you, hit them back."

"But I'll get in trouble"—though it didn't occur to me that Dino rarely did.

"If he hits you, hit him."

So I did. One day as he came sauntering up for a little light teasing, I rounded on him. I was as big as he was. Gifted the element of surprise (another fight lesson—the guy who throws first usually wins), I took him to the ground and began slamming his head into the asphalt. It was ungainly and effective. He bled, which pleased me.

I got into trouble. My mother was summoned. She reminded the principal—Sister Charlotte—that I'd been the one on the receiving end many times and nothing had come of that.

Sister Charlotte had a way explaining fights that I have never forgotten—"It takes two to tango."

Every time I'd been sent up to the office with a split lip or a torn jacket, that had been her judgment on the matter—"two to tango."

Often you ended up getting the strap—a strip of leather brought down across the open palm of your hand—alongside the guy who'd been rubbing your face in the dirt a few minutes before. That's what she called fairness.

Like those parents who tell their kids not to fight back, it's the perspective of someone who has never taken a kicking. It's the winner's point of view.

But now I was the one getting away with it. It was put down to a "boys will be boys" scenario, despite the copious blood. My mother had steered me right. If it can be said that you are friends with your parents, that's the moment it happened for me.

In the usual way of these things, Dino and I became pals after that. Not good pals. I didn't trust him, but I now understood how to handle him. You had to keep him where you could see him. Like my father. And if he came at you, you had to go back twice as hard.

Once my parents split up, my father stopped hitting me. Maybe he thought it would get him in trouble now, that there would be consequences. I was at his house most weekends. When he got angry, he'd sulk instead, or send me back to my mother. For the most part, he ignored me.

He hit me one more time, over something I can't remember. I was older then—eleven or twelve. Bigger. Already nearly as tall as him. He slapped me and I punched him in the face and time stopped.

We stood there panting in his living room, staring at each other. There was no question of me winning. He was a hard man. He'd have taken me apart easily.

But he could see that if he came at me, I was not going to stop. He'd have to put me in hospital. So he demurred.

There's another fight lesson—the person who is willing to go the furthest and do the most unthinkable things wins. It doesn't matter how big, skilled or overmatched he is. Toughness will out. The hardest guys I've ever known were little, wiry people. They won because they put their finish line at a distance the other guy could not conceive of reaching. They had mastered themselves.

Mike Tyson once said, "Fear is your best friend or your worst enemy. It's like fire. If you can control it, it can cook for you; it can heat your house. If you can't control it, it will burn everything around you and destroy you."

That's the core mantra of fighting, from someone who would know.

My mother had been right. My father never hit me again after that.

Like I had once been, my brother was systematically bullied in his grade seven year. He got it worse, from a gang of older kids who went to the public grade school adjacent to our Catholic one. There were many long-running feuds between those schools. They had the salutary effect of redirecting our animus away from our classmates and onto an "Other" as we got older.

I'd long since graduated. I gave my brother the same advice our mother had given me—hit back. But he was smaller and there were more of them.

My mother caught me in the middle of one of these useless pep talks. I may have been trying to show him how to throw a punch (as if I knew myself, which I didn't).

When my brother left, my mother got right up on top of me, chin in my chest, and said, "What are you going to do about this?"

I had no idea. What was she asking?

"I want you to find them and hurt them."

Stupidly, I went back to the "this'll mean trouble" excuse.

"He's your brother. You have to protect him. That's your job. Find them and get them."

Well, I thought, as long as I have parental permission.

I wrangled up a bunch of my friends, who were delighted at the prospect of constructing some sort of ambush. My brother gave us the route. As Dino once had, my brother's tormentors regularly followed him home. We skipped our last class and waited around a corner for Brendan to arrive. Five minutes after the bell, he came steaming around the bend, eyes wide, voice cracking, close to tears.

"They're coming! They're coming! Right now!"

I was stunned at the sight of him. I had never seen him scared or vulnerable.

Of course, he and I fought. We fought constantly, like cats in too close a proximity. On a couple of occasions, we'd really hurt each other. But there was no fear in it. Both of us understood our fights had limits. They would end and life would resume as normal. When you are afraid, you can't see that. You think the worst is always just about to happen. That sort of fear corrodes your soul.

Seeing him infected with it enraged me.

The plan had been to shake these kids up, shoot a little scare into them. They were two or three years younger than us, weaker. It wasn't a fair fight. But as they came around the corner—a little posse of four or five of them, smug looks on their faces, predatory—I lost control. I ran up and smashed the first one I saw in the face. He fell. The others froze, confused. My friends, working on my cue, descended on them like wolves. They were all on the ground, writhing, within seconds. Getting the boots. Having their backpacks opened and the contents scattered about. People on top of them screaming in their faces.

One of them was wearing a coonskin cap—an anachronistic touch even back then. My friend Jimmy took it as a trophy and afterward wore it often. When I see him now in my mind's eye, it is impossible to do it without picturing that ridiculous hat tipped over his right eye.

The bullies were down on the ground, whimpering, begging. One wet his pants. My brother was standing off to the side, gulping air.

"Which one is in charge?" I asked him.

My brother pointed to the biggest kid. The little prick was crying. His lips were caked in snot. I picked him off the ground, got hold of his hair, turned his face toward Brendan, leaned in so that we were cheek-to-cheek and said, "That's my brother. If you ever touch him again, I will find out where you live and come there and kill you."

And that was that. They didn't just stop bothering my brother. He told me later that he'd never seen them again. They'd found another way to get home. It was an awful thing to do and I don't think I've ever felt as proud. This was family. This is what it meant to be together in something. Really, truly together.

My mother never asked about it. As ever, she knew without having to ask.

In high school, fighting had become sport for us. It was a way of testing ourselves and each other. I think we did it so that we had something to bind us together. It was a military impulse that had no outlet in the civilized world of school or work. Four or five of us would have a bunch to drink in a park and strut up and down Bloor Street after dark, longing for someone to look at us funny.

I'd spend the week looking forward to these late-night prowlings.

We were thuggish, but we weren't bullies. We didn't single people out. We wanted an even fight with someone who was up for it. Even when you're sixteen, that's not easy to find. The resulting skirmishes were rare and didn't amount to much.

We'd run into an equally numbskulled band of teenagers. Someone would say something as the groups passed. Everyone turned to eye each other. There would be a bunch of "What the fuck are you looking at?" and "You want to go?"

Another fight lesson—the guy who is doing most of the talking is going to lose. Because he doesn't really want to fight. He's hoping that tough talk is enough to spare him his blushes.

At most, there'd be pushing and shoving, a few punches that didn't connect, people running toward each other like a flock of swallows diving toward ground, then pulling back at the last instant. After a few seconds, we'd use the first distraction—an over-interested passing adult or the sound of a siren in the distance—as an excuse to back away, taunting each other from a distance. This childish pantomime made us feel tough. We were ridiculous.

One of us was tough, though—Isaac. He was that proto-typical little guy—maybe five foot six, 140 pounds. He had a wild rage in him that, once released, could not be contained. His adoptive parents had put him in taekwondo as a way to channel his relentlessness, and Isaac put those years of practice to use on the street. He moved well, with economy. Fast, disciplined people often look like they're going slow, because they know where they're headed. He didn't waste energy. Mostly, he didn't believe he could lose. So he didn't.

I once saw him kick a guy five inches taller than he was square in the side of the head. The guy dropped like a tree and we ran off.

Isaac was a good guy, gentle and funny. He laughed a lot. I

never once saw him treat a friend with anything but kindness. But if you made the mistake of asking for it, he would give you a lot more than you expected. I wanted to be that. More to the point, I wanted to be seen that way—as someone who could but chose not to.

I developed a theory about fighting as it applies to men— that once in your life, you should very badly lose a fight, and on another occasion, very handily win one. The first teaches you humility; the second gives you dignity. Having done both, you can move on to a life without violence.

In the best case, it would happen in that order—lose, then win. I worked it the other way around.

The fight I won was on one of those tipsy marches. Three of us were walking down Jane Street. A car reversed too quickly out of a laneway behind the subway station, nearly hitting my friend Ned.

Ned was holding a can of pop. He threw it at the driver's side window. The car stopped. A guy hopped out of the passenger seat.

"Who the fuck threw that?"

Ned was not particularly tough, but he was enormous. Six foot five, 250 pounds. Huge.

When Ned said, "Me," that didn't seem to rattle this guy. He was in his twenties—an adult. Not big or small. Not remarkable in any way, except that he did not seem worried about the fact that there was one of him and three of us. The driver didn't say anything or move to help. He advanced the car so that it wasn't straddling the sidewalk and sat there.

"You wanna fucking go?" the guy said to Ned.

"I'll go with you," I said.

Fights happen fast. You don't get a chance to think about them. That's what the talking is—a way to delay the action so that your good sense can catch up to current events.

This guy was all business. He led me back into the alley. It was dusk on the street, but already dark in there.

"I'm going to hurt you so bad. You're going to fucking regret this," he said as we walked.

I was bigger than him. Why was he so sure of himself? There was a woman in the back seat of the car. She had her head stuck out the window, yelling at my opponent.

"Just leave it," she said. "He's a kid. Just leave it."

She sounded more annoyed than upset. Like she knew how this was going to turn out. I'd had far too long to think about this. I was awash in fear.

We got deep into the alley. We turned toward each other and squared up.

Then he turned back toward the car and started to say, "Make sure the other two don't fucking . . ."

And I kicked him in the balls. It was dead on target. It was the sort of blow that, in the normal course of events, would put you down on the ground until someone took pity and dragged you to an emergency room.

He folded, but he didn't stop. He rushed me, hitting me at waist level and taking me into a wall. That was a poor decision on his part. My hands were free and he now had no way of protecting himself.

Fuelled by terror, I began striking him in the side, in his ribs. Big, weighted hammer blows. The first two took the remaining fight out of him. As I landed the third, I heard a snap and my fist sank sickeningly into his side. He let go of me and puddled to the floor.

The woman was now out of the car, crying, running toward him.

I was shaky but managed to walk back to the sidewalk without stumbling. I didn't feel heroic. What I felt was better than that—the thrill of having survived.

It would be useful information for the fight I lost.

That one started out as so many of our phony gang fights had. A few of us, a few of them, kids we didn't recognize. Not locals. Passing on the street. A sneer or a look that someone didn't like. Words exchanged.

But, crucially, no fight started. Instead, we kept jawing. There were five of us and maybe the same number of them.

The two groups began to move in unison, down a pathway that led into Jane subway station. We roamed through the bus terminal. There were more of them now. Ten or twelve. Where were they coming from? It wasn't possible to say. Guys were materializing from hallways and off the street.

By now, we were in the road where the buses entered. It was late. There wasn't anyone else around. We were surrounded. Twenty of them now to our five.

Someone on my side had the good idea that only two people would fight—one of them and one of us. Shades of the Siege of Troy.

I volunteered. The first guy to put his hand up from their group was obviously overcome by irrational exuberance. He was half my size, scrawny. Not a tough little guy. Just a little guy.

Looking back on it, I should've thrown that fight. It might've calmed the situation before it got out of hand. I certainly should not have begun banging his head into a phone pole once I had the upper hand. And I most certainly should not have picked his baseball cap off the ground, put it on my own head and begun taunting the rest of his gang once he crumpled. That's when they fell upon us.

Yet another thing they don't tell you about fights—they are timeless.

I can't say how long that beating went on. It moved a considerable distance. By the end, we were up on Jane Street, two or three blocks from where it had started. That must've taken a while. The five of us were trying to make an orderly retreat, jogging backward like a football drill.

There were more of them now. I couldn't tell how many, maybe twenty or thirty. One of them had a mini-crowbar. I saw him flash it. Another had a length of chain. I didn't catch sight of that, but afterward you could see the marks it left across my back, flaying the t-shirt I was wearing.

We managed to escape only so far. They were after me. My friends—Ned, Ronan, Brian and John—could have run off. But they stayed to protect me, trying to act as peacemakers. There was no point in fighting back.

I moved off the sidewalk and into the middle of the road, on the theory that this could not continue with cars driving by. But it did. Nobody stopped. They only slowed before driving past. They were coming in from all angles now, hitting me from behind.

The guy with the crowbar struck me across the side of the face, cracking my jaw. Once I fell, they got on top of me, a half-dozen of them, kicking and punching. Brian tried to lie across my back, yelling, "He's done. He's done," but someone pulled him off and it started again.

No one was coming to save us.

Ned found the way out. He peeled off from the mob, grabbed a garbage can off the sidewalk and hurled it through a front window. That got someone to pick up the phone.

How long was I down there on the ground? A minute? Ten? I had no idea.

It ended when we heard the sirens. They ran off. We ran in the opposite direction. I couldn't see straight. Brian was dragging me up the street when the first cop car—an unmarked cruiser—mounted the sidewalk.

A pudgy guy in a t-shirt and jeans came screaming out and grabbed hold of me. A good thing, because I couldn't stand on my own. My shirt was ripped completely down the front. I was covered in blood. Strangely, the first thing he was interested in was my teeth. He stuck his fingers in my mouth to check that I still had them.

I reached to pat him on the sides in a reassuring gesture and felt the gun on his belt.

"You're a cop?" I said.

"Yes."

"I'm okay. I'm okay. I'm not pressing charges."

It must have been the stupidity of the comment that caught him off guard. He got back in the car and left.

I walked home. I looked like I'd been put through a windshield, but I had no sense of that. All I wanted now was revenge.

The front door of our house opened into the living room. My mother and brother were sitting on the couch watching a movie when I came in. My brother yelped. My mother was pinned to her seat.

"Where's my baseball bat?"

Nobody spoke.

"The bat? The aluminum one? Have you seen it?"

Still silence.

"Oh, wait. I think I left it in the basement."

I went downstairs, got the bat, came back up. They were still frozen on the couch.

"I'll be back soon," I said, and left again.

In a small miracle, nothing else happened that night. I wandered around until my head cleared a little. Then it dawned on me that a bat wasn't going to do me much good against two dozen guys. So I went home.

My mother was waiting for me, as close to frantic as she ever got (which was not very). She was too relieved to be angry. I went to bed. In the morning, one side of my face was so swollen I couldn't open my mouth properly for weeks.

For a long time, I kept the t-shirt I'd been wearing. It had been grey, but it turned black after being soaked through with blood.

By the time I lost track of it, it was hard to remember the last time I'd been in a fight.

TELEVISION

MY MOTHER HIT ME only twice in my life.

The second time was in mistaken self-defence. We were in the midst of one of the raging arguments that typified my early teenage years.

Like so many of them, I couldn't say what it was about. Where I'd been? Who I'd been with? The screaming match was moving through our small bungalow. I tried to storm off into the room I shared with my brother and I didn't realize my mother had run in directly behind me.

As I swung around to make a theatric "And one *other* thing . . ." gesture, she ducked under my raised arm, bobbed back up like Sugar Ray Robinson and nailed me in the chin with an uppercut. There wasn't much force in the blow, but it was a square shot.

I landed on my bed and lay there for a while. My mother was breathing heavily, shoulders curled, ready.

"I wasn't trying to hit you," I said.

"You better not," she said.

Hostilities ceased temporarily since, out in the hallway, my brother had burst into tears. We never mentioned it again.

After that, our shrieking arguments shifted to a more civil, smouldering model, which involved fewer punches but more cutting comments, followed by long silences. In the fullest consideration, it wasn't an improvement.

The first time she hit me, she meant it. It was over television.

If you were a kid in the 1970s, TV was a towering monoculture. You may have done other things, but TV was the only one of them that you knew to a certainty you shared with your peers. It was a childhood lingua franca.

It was also your gateway to the reality outside your house. You got all your news from the television. It shaped your taste. It armed you with all of your metaphors.

I still understand romantic relationships with reference to *The Flintstones*. Because Fred and Wilma had a marriage that should not have worked. Yet somehow it did. That's hopeful.

Every episode was framed around some conniving on one or the other's part, terrible consequences because of that, an unlikely solution and concluding exclamations of love and devotion. Every single episode. These people never learned anything, and yet never suffered for their pettiness and ignorance. Even at seven years old, this merited serious thought.

Fortunately, the only thing you had to occupy your time when you weren't watching TV was thinking about TV. Like, how would one patch the hull of a boat after crashing on a deserted shore? It was clear from the opening credits of *Gilligan's Island* that the SS *Minnow* had two large holes in its undercarriage. Could we presume that there would be some sort of toolbox on board? Yes, we could, because the Professor wasn't building those chemistry sets—complete with bamboo beakers—using rocks.

Could we further surmise that materials for repair were at hand? Well, yes, because the Howells had constructed a cottage, complete with terrace.

The expertise? It's reasonable to assume that a skipper has some experience of boat construction. If not, what about a raft? Wouldn't a raft do the trick? Like, I could build a raft. Right now. It'd take me a day. Two, max. They were on that island for years. They'd been on it as long as I'd been alive.

Didn't they want to leave? Why wasn't that their only goal? Had they succumbed to despair?

And surely you couldn't survive forever on coconuts and gin fizz? Wasn't scurvy a thing? Why weren't they hunting? When would they go feral?

We considered these issues without irony. They were honest problems with honest answers, if only you could figure them out. While we knew this was make-believe, we were still kids and hadn't mentally graduated to the concept of whimsy. We couldn't see that not solving the problem was a way of solving a different, far-more-important problem—how to keep a show with one flimsy premise and six jokes (skipper melts down; Howells befuddled; movie star pouts; farm girl ignored; professor book-learned and witless; Gilligan stumbles on solution) on the air for two decades.

We ate lunch at the house of our babysitter, a saintly woman named Mrs. Spiteri.

Over the years, Mrs. Spiteri had as many as a half-dozen kids under her watch at any given time. They were all ages. Over the years, I went from one of the youngest to the oldest.

I wasn't in Mrs. Spiteri's care, as such. Out of necessity, I'd been minding myself after school since my parents separated. I only showed up for a free meal.

We were allowed into only one room of her house—a kitchen the size of a walk-in closet. The dining room and living room were maintained in better order than a museum exhibit— all the furniture sheathed in plastic. Those rooms were a forbidden zone and though I saw into them every day for years, I never once crossed their threshold.

With all these kids penned in one small area, Mrs. Spiteri maintained order through cunning use of a television. We'd tramp in after noon, wedge together thickly around a Formica table and be directed toward a small black-and-white TV set perched on one edge.

"Watch," she'd say. "Quiet. Watch."

Along with "Eat" and "Go," those were her only instructions.

She was one of those gentle people who rule by moral suasion. She never raised her voice. She had that rare ability to make commands sound like requests. In a different time and world, she could have a run a country.

We weren't allowed to touch the dial. We watched whatever was on.

The only thing that was ever on was *Gilligan's Island*. We'd get there halfway into one repeat, and get halfway through the beginning of another.

We didn't talk to each other. We watched, shovelled food for twenty minutes and then we left. When I got home after school I turned on *Gilligan's Island* and watched it again, often the same episode. I know the textual references of *Gilligan's Island* more completely than any Oxford scholar can know Shakespeare. I was one of millions of such experts.

At home, we had the run of the TV. As a rule, my mother never sat in front of it. She'd been raised on a farm without a television and had no interest in being seduced by one now. The only thing we watched together as a family was the marriage of Charles and Diana. I had mumps at the time and was swollen up like a blowfish. Nevertheless, my mother dragged me out of bed at five in the morning on a weekend to attend the festivities. It was so much an event in our house that my mother brought out the camera and we took pictures of each other.

Like everyone else in our family, my mother despised the Royals. They represented everything we did not have—the ability and resources to float above the troubles of real life.

Also like everyone else in our family, my mother was obsessed with the Royals. She'd occasionally rail about them—the Queen's Christmas address was an annual target. No winter holiday was complete without a rundown of what the Queen had said and why all of it was rank hypocrisy. She couldn't bring herself to watch it live. She read the text in the next day's paper.

During Diana's wedding, I was more interested in watching my mother watching it than I was in anything that was going on. At points, she was close to tears. This was an early lesson in how people are complicated. Even my mother. Maybe more than most.

During the time I was in grade school, there were two varieties of TV—Canadian (i.e., bad) TV and American (i.e., good) TV.

Everybody got Canadian TV. It required no additional equipment. You turned on the set and there they were—the leafy greens of television, informative and good for your development.

It was also cheap and banal. Banal in this achingly, well-intentioned Canadian way.

The first issue was presentation. All Canadian TV looked the same—flat and overlit, like someone had set up a spotlight behind the camera. Cop shows, kids' shows, soap opera knock-offs—they all had an identical, washed-out palette.

The second issue was narrative. Canadian auteurs were determined to make TV from topics of the least possible interest. For a long while, the big show was *The Beachcombers*. It was an adventure story about logging. Really. That was it. They gunned up the coast and logged. People were forever jumping in boats because some logs were headed their way.

Why are Canadians so good at satire? Because in the Canadian language, "drama" is the more correct way of saying "comedy."

I didn't know anything about anything, but I knew in my bones that this was second-rate stuff. There had to be something better. That was American TV. It got beamed in across the border from Buffalo, New York, a magical place in my mind that would remain so until I went there and learned the truth. To access American TV, you needed cable. We didn't have cable. We couldn't afford it.

I begged my mother for cable. Her rejoinder? "When are you getting a real job?"

I was ten. I had a job, delivering newspapers after school. But I didn't care to share my earnings around for something that obviously fell under the accounting line of "Adult Expenses."

My father didn't have cable either. The one time I asked him about it, he took the same "get a job" position as my mother.

This is where I might've said, "I have a job. What about you?" but that seemed unwise.

This lack of cable nagged at me, but I'd learned to live around it. When other kids talked about shows they were watching on American TV, I'd nod along thoughtfully and say things like, "That was so good" and "I can't wait for next week."

Then *V* happened.

V was a three-part miniseries about an alien invasion that aired in 1983. It was my first experience of event television—something that would happen only once, briefly, like a comet passing overhead, and then be entirely inaccessible for all the rest of time.

You had one chance at *V*. After that, there would be two types of people in the world—those who had seen *V* and those who did not matter.

Other American TV didn't bother me because you heard about those shows after they'd aired. There was no point in regretting something that had already happened.

But *V* got massive publicity in the run-in. The schoolyard was abuzz with it.

I didn't bother asking for cable again because cable had grown so large in my mind that I imagined the installation process was akin to building a third floor on your house. Something as incredible as cable must take months to set up. There must be dozens of workmen involved. It was already too late.

After the first episode, kids would come to school early just to talk about it. And it sounded *fucking amazing*. It was the greatest thing that had ever happened. Like you were there at the birth of Christ, but with aliens.

There was a bit in it where one of the aliens—who look indistinguishable from people but are lizards in disguise—eats a hamster. Puts it in her mouth and eats it. Nobody had ever done anything that interesting on *The King of Kensington*.

The hamster detail crushed me. Someone asked if I'd seen it and I was forced to pretend I had.

"Yes! Of course! Gross!" I squealed, withering inside.

I could have gone to a friend's house to watch *V*, but that would have meant admitting our no-cable shame. I had my pride.

But really, what was the point? Why go on? It would never get any better than this, and I'd been at home watching *The Littlest Hobo*.

My despair moved my mother. Or maybe she got a little bump in pay. Who knows? But a few months after that, she folded. There was no preamble, no preparatory celebrations. One morning my mother said someone was coming over to install cable and it happened like that.

I was embittered and beyond caring. Where was this guy when I needed him? It was too late now.

The cable guy showed up and fiddled around outside the house for a bit. We stood in the living room, staring at the TV like a stone idol.

He came back in, plugged in a remote the size of a phone book and turned the TV on. Static. He turned the dials. Nothing.

I knew it. I fucking knew it. There was something wrong with our house. Cable would never happen here. Could not happen here. It was a cosmic prank.

The workman went outside again.

I wheeled on my mother and shrieked, "Nothing good ever happens to us."

And she slapped me. A good, hard, open palm across the face.

When the workman came back in, the three of us were standing there dumbly, staring at each other. I felt enraged and ashamed. My mother was trembling. My brother was about to cry.

The workman said something like, "I think that'll do it," turned the TV back and on and voila—cable. Then he left.

I suppose this is where I should say something about the disappointment of getting the things that you want, but that would be another lie. Cable was even better than I'd dreamed. It was a bridge into a better, more professionally lit world.

I arranged my life around the broadcast schedule—*Family Ties*; *Miami Vice*; *The A-Team*; *Magnum P.I.*; *Knight Rider*. I spent entire days doing nothing but watching music videos. I spent many hundreds of hours in front of the TV and I regret not one minute of it. I suppose I might've been downhill skiing or building my own computer, but I don't like those things. We waste far too much time worrying about what we should have been doing at the expense of enjoying whatever we did. I refuse to play that game.

(I did eventually watch *V* on VHS. It's horrendous schlock and I would still give anything to be able to go back and see it as it aired in real time.)

Most of my TV life is a big blur of multi-cam sitcoms, news broadcasts and baseball games, except for the day we watched the space shuttle *Challenger* disaster at Mrs. Spiteri's house.

It was 1986. I was in grade eight. The shuttle itself was no longer a big deal. They'd been running it up into space for nearly five years at that point. It never seemed to do anything up there except float around grabbing things. But that launch was an event because of Christa McAuliffe, a New Hampshire schoolteacher who'd been chosen to participate as a sort of "citizen astronaut." The spacecraft exploded live on television just over a minute after takeoff.

I remember that day perfectly. I remember where I was sitting when it happened—crowded in around Mrs. Spiteri's kitchen table. I remember the sound in the room when it happened—silence; Mrs. Spiteri detaching herself from her habitual pose over the stove to come over and whisper something in Maltese while crossing herself. I remember my brother, still only ten years old and therefore a hopeless optimist, saying, "They're okay, right?"

I ran back to school to talk about it and found that I was breaking the news. Most of my friends ate in the lunchroom in the basement. They hadn't heard a thing.

Nobody would believe me. It was too incredible. I was making it up.

But after we got back into class, the principal made a PA system announcement about the accident and we said a prayer. While everybody bowed their head, I looked around the room feeling a smug sense of vindication. It's ended up being a happy memory of a bad thing.

It's seldom that you get the chance to match a distant memory of childhood directly against the historical record. Perishingly few things register that deeply. When I went back to check what I recall against the indisputable record, there were discrepancies.

The shuttle blew up at 11:36 a.m. EST. That's a fact.

At 11:36 a.m., I would still have been at my desk in Ms. Florio's class. The lunch bell didn't go until noon. The walk to Mrs. Spiteri's took about ten minutes.

Evidently, what I remember is a replay of the explosion. That's why the channel wasn't on *Gilligan's Island* or *Happy Days*. They'd interrupted regularly scheduled broadcasting. Mrs. Spiteri must have already known it had happened.

Did she still cross herself, then? Maybe. Did my brother still wonder if the astronauts had survived? Possibly. But given that

I've got other things wrong, very possibly not. While I've spent three decades collecting this memory, my subconscious has been rewriting it. Not changing it entirely, but applying a series of corrective tweaks. Replacing good lines with better ones, inserting people on the periphery who weren't there, monkeying with the timeline.

However it actually went, my mind has retroactively put me there as it happened, rather than just after. How many of my other memories have shifted in this way? How much of what I believe happened is an approximation of events rather than a documentary record?

You don't recall your life as a broad sweep of events. It isn't a two-hour film with a beginning, middle and end. Instead, it's a series of random snapshots. They have a cinematic clarity—who was standing where, what they said and what you said back.

At best, these small moments are interconnected vignettes that, were you to shuffle them into the right order, might make a decent art film. It's probable only you would get it.

BASEBALL

IF YOU GREW UP IN TORONTO in the seventies and eighties, it was hard to love the Blue Jays. They had no stars. They were no good. They played in what was functionally an industrial site with the concrete floor painted green. They were the Leafs minus the history.

Now the Expos—that team was pure (platonic) sports sex. Tim Raines, Gary Carter, Andre Dawson. Several of them were raging cokeheads, which in retrospect just makes them seem cooler.

Think back to every time you've done drugs. Now picture yourself wheeling out of the bathroom to find the living room suddenly filled with thirty thousand people. You're standing there in pyjamas and a guy is launching ninety-mile-an-hour projectiles at your head. That's talent.

The Expos were rock stars. The Jays were an unusually fit branch of the pipefitters' union.

I came to the Blue Jays in reverse. It wasn't the team that interested me at first, but the mechanics of the game.

At the time, the local paper would run all the statistics of every major league player once a week. Two pages of them, tightly spaced. This was life perfectly ordered—who was good and who was bad. There was no arguing with this arrangement of numbers. Its internal logic was ruthless and consistent.

There are all sorts of reasons that people give over so much of their time and consideration to pro sports—tribalism, escapism, the vicarious thrill of watching better men do things you can't. But I believe the root of it is that sports are the closest we come to a meritocracy.

You can fake your way through most things in life. It's been my experience that the most successful people are usually the most adept phonies. There's no harm in it, I suppose. Working life is a competition. Some adapt to it better than others, and have earned the spoils.

That was another one of my mother's mantras—don't complain. Nobody cares and it doesn't change anything. Every time someone tells me about so-and-so having gotten what they have unfairly, I picture all the zebras down at the watering hole moaning about the lions.

Schoolyards, schools and jobs are unfair places. You don't get what you think you deserve.

That doesn't happen in baseball. You are exactly as good as your batting average. No more, no less and no use in whining about it. Doesn't matter if you're ugly or unpopular or a complete goddamned weirdo. If you can hit the ball, you're in. If you can't, it's your own fault.

That was the appeal of baseball for me. It was fair.

I have never watched much baseball. The games were interminably long and the stakes were too often small. But I enjoyed reading about it. I liked collecting the information.

Someone had given me a Maury Wills book on the hundred greatest players of all time—a series of thumbnail sketches. I pored dozens of times over No. 1—Hank Aaron.

Imagine being the best—the very best—at something. Of all time. And having the numbers to prove it.

I memorized career batting averages and home run totals. I learned how to score a game by hand.

My mother would occasionally take us to a game at the old Exhibition Stadium—a decrepit football facility ill suited to baseball. The seats were always miles away from the plate. You couldn't see what was going on. Regardless of the season, it was cold. More often than not, the Jays lost.

Most disappointingly, none of the players were iconic in the way Hank Aaron was. At best, the contrary part of me enjoyed being part of a lost cause.

I still had a Gary Carter poster on the wall, but the Jays got better and I bought in. By 1985, they were good. They won the division and made the playoffs for the first time.

For Thanksgiving that year, my father's family had their one and only reunion. There were twelve brothers and sisters. There were so many kids in the Kelly family they had spares. They'd given a daughter away to a childless relation as they left Ireland. There were dozens more people connected as cousins.

Whenever my father's immediate family gathered in a group, it fell to fighting. That was inevitable. Things would go well for a while. Then everyone had a few drinks. Then someone said something to Frank about Noreen, which was filtered through Kathleen. Frank got upset. Sean got involved. Finnan tried to bust it up. (The names and roles here—Donal, Michael, Emer,

Deidre—were interchangeable.) Then the shouting. Then the general scrum.

It never quite got to fisticuffs, but it was always close.

At this point of greatest danger, someone would set to wailing, "This is killing Mammy!"

Mammy, my grandmother, was a small, inoffensive woman. She spoke in a tremulous whisper. There was a soft whistle in her words, an especially sibilant *s*. Even in the most mundane situations, she seemed forever on the verge of tears.

My grandfather died before I was born. He was apparently a cartoonish brute. This conferred upon my grandmother a saintliness particular to Irish mothers who've suffered. There was a tragic intensity about her that, even as a boy, I found hard to bear. I could never quite meet her eyes.

Just as her adult children and their spouses were set to begin battering each other at a Canada Day barbecue, my grandmother would be produced. There was a great theatricality to this gesture that everyone understood. The crowd would part and she would appear—James Brown–style, being led by one of her sons.

"Please," she'd say, and all the men would hang their heads in shame. The women would run to her. That was it—"Please." She'd circle the group, touching each one on the shoulder and gently moving him or her away from the incipient fray.

A new fight would break out about who was most at fault for upsetting Mammy, but it was half-hearted. Then we'd all go home. Weeks or months later, they'd all pretend they hadn't done this before, and do it again.

The reunion was held at my aunt Deidre's house in North Bay. She was the one who'd remained there and married a French Canadian named Armand. They'd done well for themselves.

They were the only ones with a spread suitable to host a hundred people.

I'd driven up alone with my father that weekend. Deidre and Armand's house filled quickly. The party started on a Thursday and didn't flag. By Saturday night, it had morphed into a pagan ritual—bonfires in the backyard; hooting in the moonlight. They'd begun building a beer-can pyramid that reached ten feet off the ground. I didn't know half these people.

My father was engaged in one of his occasional attempts at sobriety. His mood suffered for it. He planted himself on a lawn chair and felt sorry for himself while everyone else staggered around. It was at this point that, from out of the darkness, a half-eaten chicken leg came cartwheeling at him and hit him in the face. My father popped out of the chair.

"Who threw that?" he screamed. "Who fucking threw that?"

Everyone got very quiet. There were a lot of men you didn't want to cross in that backyard, and none you wanted to cross less than my father.

Deidre lurched into view.

"I threw it," she said.

"Why?"

"I was trying to hit Armand. I wanted him to know it was good."

Imagine it being like that all the time. Because it sort of was.

As the festivities dragged on, I was getting sick. My chest was tightening. It felt as if I were breathing through a straw. The worst part about asthma is the sense of panic, the feeling that a minute or ten minutes from now you won't be able to breathe at all. Once the panic gets hold of you, you're in real trouble.

Normally, I'd have told my mother and we'd have gone to an emergency room. I told my father. He was not impressed. He wanted to know how bad it was.

"Well, bad."

"But how bad?"

"Just bad."

"Let's see how it is tomorrow." And he went back to the party.

By the next morning, it was very bad. My father was still doubtful. It's hard to argue with asthma—you can hear the wheezing and see the fevered pallor—but my father wanted to argue. How was it compared to other times? Did it ever just go away? Maybe if I sat out in the fresh air for a while. So I put on a coat and sat out on the back porch for an hour by myself. It didn't help.

I need to go to the hospital, I told him. Mom would've taken me to the hospital by now.

That annoyed him. He said we'd wait and see.

I did not want to cause a fuss, but finally I went to Deidre. She took hold of my shoulders, looked at me for a few seconds and threw a fit. She went to my father and yelled at him in front of everyone. What was he doing? Your son is sick. Go to the hospital.

So, peevishly, he took me to the hospital. We didn't talk on the way over. Once he'd checked me in and got me seated in a waiting room, he left. He told me to call once I was done. He didn't leave a phone number.

At this point, I was woozy from oxygen deprivation. The next few hours were a blur. When I snapped back to, I was in a hospital bed, hooked up to IVs. That had never happened before.

It was never made clear to me what my father had said when he'd left to take a kid to the hospital, then returned an hour later without the kid. But it was the habit of his family not to get too involved in other people's business.

No one at the hospital seemed to wonder where my parents were, and I couldn't tell them. I was in a semi-conscious state, largely because when the admitting nurse asked my father if I had any allergies, my father said, "No," having no idea if that was true or not. I did have allergies, a bunch of them. They pumped me full of a medicine I was particularly allergic to. That made me exponentially more ill.

I suppose they must have figured that out (I would only be told about it much later). The worst of it passed. I was still profoundly unwell, as sick as I'd ever been. I was still hooked up to drips and monitors. But I was alone and it was quiet. That was a nice change.

I began to think about the Blue Jays. The American League Championship series had been going on through all of this and, since my father's family had no interest in baseball, I hadn't seen any of it. There were no newspapers about. I had no idea how they were doing.

I asked a nurse about the playoffs. A few minutes later, she returned to say Toronto was winning. That evening, another nurse rolled a television into my room—one of those grade-school A/V set-ups, perched on a cart. If I was very quiet, I'd be allowed to watch the game. A great deal was made of the fact that no one else was getting this privilege. It occurred to me that I had become an object of pity. I didn't like that feeling, but if it got me a TV I was happy to play along. I tried to look especially miserable.

I don't know if I'd watched a complete Jays' game that whole season. I knew everything that had gone on, but through box scores. Now, lying in that hospital bed, plucked out of the world, not sure if anyone knew where I was or cared, the Jays suddenly seemed of desperate importance. In a way that is hard for me to understand now and harder still to explain, the baseball team's fortunes became intertwined with my own. If they were okay, I would be okay.

It was looking good. The Jays were up 2–1 in a best-of-seven series.

I groggily watched Game 4 in that bed. The Jays won. Al Oliver had the big hit in the ninth.

Oliver was a thirty-eight-year-old journeyman at the end of his professional road. When he'd been traded to the Jays earlier in the season, I'd checked the numbers—shabby. But he was a monster in that playoff series.

I hadn't cared that much about Oliver before, but he now became my personal avatar. Al Oliver was doing this for me. I daydreamed that in a *Diff'rent Strokes*-ian twist, he was my father. I pretended that I'd been the one who'd believed in him all along. Al and me—the redoubtables. Once we got this baseball thing done and dusted, we'd head off together and have adventures. I was taking a lot of medication.

Game 5 was played on Sunday. The Jays lost. I took that with equanimity.

I'd now been in the hospital for several days. I wasn't keeping good track. No one had come to visit me. None of the nurses or doctors had bothered to tell me what was going on, probably because I didn't ask and they all assumed someone else had done it. I was okay with that.

This was my home now. I'd stay here and watch baseball until someone threw me out.

The Jays lost Game 6, and I did as well. There was a lot of yelling.

The nurses were starting to worry. They'd given me this electronic soother and couldn't really take it back now, but I was not playing nice.

First, they shut the door. Then they asked me to be quiet. Then they told me to be quiet. Then I told them to be quiet. That was the end of our warm relationship, but they let me keep the TV.

Before Game 7, I prayed.

Until this point, I had prayed the way I assume most people pray—a lot of filler up front about peace on earth and ending global hunger, with the real point of the prayer tucked in at the end: "Please give me X" or "If you have a spare moment, please kill Y in some horrible way."

I didn't expect any of my prayers to come true, but it was important to get this stuff on the record. For later.

"Yes, it's true that I've been less than perfect, but let's refer back to my long series of assassination requests in fifth grade. There's plenty of blame to go around here."

That day, I straight up begged. Let the Jays win. Let the goddamned Kansas City Royals lose. Because I hate them. Let a line drive hit George Brett in the face and permanently disfigure him. Let Al Oliver have five home runs, and then let him drive up here to whatever this hospital is called and spend the night telling me about it. Wherever You are, this will be proof that You care.

Of course, the Jays lost miserably. I wept with inconsolable anger. A nurse came in and tried to calm me down. It didn't take. Eventually, she got into the bed with me so that I would stop slamming my fists against the railings. That is the purest sports emotion I have ever felt.

My mother came to get me the following weekend. My father had returned home and hadn't bothered to call her. She'd had to phone my aunt before anyone told her where I was. Then she had to wait for her brother's day off so that someone could take her five hours north, since she couldn't drive.

I don't remember anything about her arriving. Not her coming through the door or the packing me up or the getting in a car (all things that must have happened). I don't remember any sense of rescue or relief. It had only been a few days, but days of such unaccustomed isolation that I think I'd given up on ever leaving.

I lasted a day at home before I needed to go to the hospital again. It was assumed that I'd be there for a while, so I was placed in a cystic fibrosis ward. Every day, a phalanx of attendants would come in, bend these painfully frail kids over the edge of their beds and beat the phlegm out of their lungs. Often more than once. Everyone in there spent most of their days hacking into buckets. It was medieval.

My clearest memory of the teenager in the bed alongside mine was that he had a laptop computer. I'd never even heard of such a thing.

If you want to put your troubles in perspective, spend one night with twenty kids who all know they're going to die, and soon. Nobody left that room and nobody expected to.

Every time I begin to feel sorry for myself, I think about that place. I memorized the small, brutal details for that very purpose. After North Bay, my mother went to court and my father had his visitation rights severed. He'd never paid child support and wasn't about to start now, so he didn't bother fighting and I didn't miss him.

Once I recovered, the Jays passed beyond an interest and into a fixation. From '85 until they won the World Series in 1992, the Blue Jays were the perfect sports organization. They often disappointed, but what they offered is what fans want but have trouble articulating—a chance to tease.

People learn to hate a team that is good, but not good enough. And they don't want a team that comes out of nowhere to win everything either. Not really.

What they want is a team that takes incremental steps over many years toward an inevitable goal, and then gets there. They want the slow, painful build and the cathartic pleasure of eventual release.

Those Jays did that. They taunted you with potential. They blew it in '87 and got hammered the next two times they made the playoffs in '89 and '91. In between, they opened the SkyDome and now you could see what was going on.

I'd become so used to the experience of sitting in the outer rings that I couldn't acclimate myself to the Dome's closeness. A girlfriend gave me her father's season tickets early in the '92 season. First baseline, front row. I took my brother.

We set to our usual routine of catcalling the visitors—in this case, the Detroit Tigers.

The Tigers' catcher at the time was Mickey Tettleton, a decent player who looked as if someone had stuck a bike pump in his armpit and inflated him for several hours.

In the pre-game, Tettleton walked by us with a bat hanging off his shoulder, bored out of his mind, headed down the right-field line to the visitors' bullpen.

Very few people had taken their seats at this point. We were almost alone in the stands. As Tettleton passed, we began idiotically mocking him: "Miiii-keeeee, Miiii-keeeee."

It didn't register with us that we were no longer in the nosebleeds. He could hear and see us. It was the equivalent of jeering the guy sitting across from you on the bus.

"Miiiii-keeee, Miiiii-keeee."

Tettleton stopped and swivelled. He was maybe six feet away. Running was not an option unless we split up. One of us would survive.

"What are you doing?" he said. He was more curious than angry.

"Nothing."

"Well, stop it."

"Yes, sorry. Sorry, Mickey. Have a great game! Sorry again." Then he walked away.

It was a golden time to care about baseball in Toronto and it will never be repeated. By now, the Jays had found their great stars—Roberto Alomar, Joe Carter, Tony Fernández, Jesse Barfield, George Bell. A team that had had none was now bursting with them. No Toronto team in my lifetime has had more charisma.

Years later, I was offered the chance to become the Blue Jays beat writer for the *Toronto Star*.

"Tell me one thing," the sports editor asked. "Do you follow baseball?"

"Yes, of course. Absolutely," I lied.

At the time, I couldn't name five players on the team. Back in the day, I could've told you the batting average of every man on the roster.

In 1992, the Jays won the World Series. I didn't live at home anymore, but I was there for the final game. It was the only time I remember my mother, brother and me watching an entire contest of any sort all together.

When Atlanta tied the game in the ninth, I walked out of the house and began kicking a plastic garbage can down the street. One of our neighbours came rushing out in alarm and watched me brutalize the container for a while.

"What are you doing?"

"Nothing. Sorry. Nothing."

I picked up the can and went back to the house. I told my brother to tell me what happened. Then I stood on the porch for the two extra innings. After every batter, my brother came out to let me know what had happened.

I believe strongly that you can curse a thing by depending on an outcome. So I cleared my mind of desire. Whatever would happen had, in a sense, already happened. Take yourself to that future place. This mantra has seen me through many a hard time.

When it got to two outs in the bottom of the 11th with the Jays in the lead, I came back in. I was there for the end.

We didn't hug. We weren't huggers. My mother said something about getting up early and went upstairs. My brother and I sat on the porch for a while and talked about nothing in particular. We could dimly hear people celebrating around us, the shouts coming from the main street down the block.

I took the side streets to get back to my apartment. My girlfriend was asleep, so I sat up for a while by myself in the living room thinking about '85 and how things connect.

What if the Jays had won then? Would that have changed anything for me?

No. Nothing at all. The circle was always going to close. It just took a while. In the meantime, it had given me something outside myself to focus on.

I stopped watching baseball then. It had served its purpose.

THE MICHAEL JACKSON JACKET

A FEW YEARS AGO, a travelling exhibit of David Bowie's collected paraphernalia came through town. When I was young, Bowie was just another pop star. I came to him too late—in his "Let's Dance" phase—to be an acolyte. Everyone I went to school with liked him. No one loved him. He was no different than Thomas Dolby or Howard Jones or any other vaguely fashionable purveyor of smart (i.e., British) synth music.

Now that I am old and he is dead, Bowie has graduated to cultural prophet, a sort of boomer Jesus. All the things people held against him at the time—the overweening artistry, the androgyny, the sly, distant persona, the refusal to settle on a style and churn out hits—have become, in retrospect, indications of his saintliness.

It's proof that you have to choose—be seen as right now, or be proven right later.

Two things struck me at that show.

First, David Bowie was small. Like, elfin. I couldn't wear his pants as arm sleeves. This is why I never dreamed of being a rock star—I had to accept that I was too fat to fit into the job. Also, I couldn't sing or play an instrument or dance in any way that didn't look like I was in the midst of a fit.

I believe this is why hip hop has become the monolithic musical genre of the modern age—it can be performed by normal-looking people in jeans from the husky section, rather than by hipless, Mick Jagger–looking people in spandex.

The second thing that hit me was the clothes. Bowie wasn't there, of course. His clothes stood in for him, fitted onto mannequins.

With several decades of his wardrobe on hand, you did not feel the absence of the man who'd owned it. As with everyone, his body had changed over the years. He'd caked on more or less make-up, had different hairstyles, had his tombstone teeth torn out and replaced with a Chiclet smile (a terrible decision)

But if you had pinned up a series of Bowie's portraits through the course of his career, it would not have told you as much about him as what he wore.

For Bowie—and maybe for all of us—fashion is reality.

Children in the twenty-first century are fashionable. I've noticed this. They look put together. Like they've stood on a stool in the bathroom with a couple of polos on hangers, flashing them in front of the mirror to see which one goes better with teal.

This is one of the notable modern victories of the marketing-industrial complex—convincing six-year-olds that how they look matters.

We did not care how we looked. We were not fashionable. Our mothers bought our clothes. Going back over the photo evidence, they bought them without an iota of thought put into how the clothes would look on us. Every grade-school class photo looks like it was taken at a down-at-heel jockey academy—a lot of tartan, checks and polka dots. Nothing fit right. The shirts were too big or far too small. Everyone got their pants at the Polyester Emporium.

Our mothers had two rules of fashion: our clothes were cheap and non-flammable. There was a lot more fire in the seventies.

I was especially unaware of how I projected myself into the world. It wasn't that I didn't think about it. It was that I didn't realize you could.

The only item I can recall with any specificity from my childhood was a dishdasha that an aunt and uncle had brought back from Lebanon. They'd gone there on what had seemed an impossibly cheap overseas holiday. When the front door to the hotel was blown off in a bombing, they began to understand why.

The dishdasha was, depending on your perspective, a charming example of exotic finery or a dress for men. I was only allowed to wear it in the house, which shows you on which side my mother fell. She was open-minded, but the aperture only widened so far.

What I do remember is the first item of clothing I wanted. In the best tradition of going hard on the way in, at age twelve I fixed myself on Michael Jackson's jacket.

Everyone liked *Thriller*. Because if you didn't, life would not have been bearable. That album and every song off it were in constant rotation for the better part of two years. *Thriller* was more the soundtrack of our lives than the hymns at church or the national anthem we sang every morning.

My ur-image of Jackson—the one I wanted to steal for myself—was taken from his "Beat It" video. In it, he wears the most ridiculous garment ever conceived.

There have been down moments in fashion through history. The kilt, for instance. That makes no sense. It's a bolt of cloth you wrap around yourself. It's fabric that has *not yet been turned into clothes*. It's like pushing yourself around on a wooden wheel because you don't have time to wait for it to be attached to a wagon. That's the kilt. But people wear it.

French aristocrats used to style their hair around birdcages, with birds in them. That's not just imbecilic. It's unhygienic. But the best way to visibly separate yourself from the plebs is to wear something they have neither the time, money nor inclination to put on themselves. You can't go down the coal mine with a live crow knotted into your ponytail, for instance.

The "Beat It" jacket was in that same tradition—fire-engine red, chainmail at the shoulders, covered in non-functional zippers. I did not yet understand the distinction between clothing and costume. This was the latter.

Jackson's "Thriller" jacket—the one with the stylized *M* that made him look like a particularly progressive member of the space program—is more iconic. People are still trying to copy that coat. But the "Beat It" jacket is purer Jackson because it is more definably kitsch.

A Versailles courtier would have thought it just a bit too much, but I wanted it.

Certain ridiculous items of clothing creep into the mainstream for a moment—say, drop-crotch pants or platform boots. This wasn't one of those. Everyone knew the "Beat It" jacket, but no one wore it. No one.

I would blaze that trail. I spotted one in a shop window at the Eaton Centre, where I spent most Saturday afternoons wandering around aimlessly with friends. I don't remember what it cost, but it wasn't cheap. It took me months to save up the money from my paper route. I could have held on to that stash for a couple of years and bought Apple stock. If I had, I'd be writing these words from inside the cockpit of my private helicopter as it sat down on the south lawn of my Tuscan villa. The smaller one.

But, as usual, I wasn't thinking too far ahead.

I didn't tell anyone about my plan. It was the first time I'd "shopped" without my mother. I didn't understand the codes of commerce. That you have to find someone to show you whatever it is you want, and do the dance of considering buying it. I just walked into the store and tried to pull the coat off the rack. When someone intercepted me, I tried handing him the money.

The most notable part of the transaction was that the guy who sold me the jacket spent the better part of ten minutes trying to talk me out of the purchase.

"Are you sure about this?" he said. He was young, but clearly sophisticated. He must have been. He was wearing leather pants.

In retrospect, I should have bought those instead. It would have been the only time in my life I could fit into a pair.

I told him I was sure.

"Why?"

"I really like Michael Jackson."

"Yes, but . . . ," he said, regarding me sadly. It should have bothered me more that he didn't finish the thought.

I was so excited that I wore it home on the subway. For the first time in my life, strangers noticed me. People asked about it or yelled out "JACKSON!" as I walked by. I did not enjoy that feeling. They weren't making fun, as such—I was too small to be freely mocked. But it did not feel as if I was being admired.

When I showed it to my mother, she got a look on her face. She knew. But it wasn't in her nature to offer an opinion in a matter of taste. She had a Catholic farm girl's take on haberdashery— it was meant to cover your nakedness and protect you from the elements. As long as it accomplished those two goals, how it looked didn't matter.

I wore the jacket to school on Monday. I'm not sure what I expected would happen. I might have hoped for a few admiring comments. But I didn't want it to be a big deal.

It was a big deal.

Kids gathered around in a circle to touch it. The girls wanted to wear it (another bad sign). Someone asked how much it had cost and when I told them, people laughed. There was a lot of laughing. Not the good kind.

I went home in it and on the way a bunch of older kids I didn't know pointed in a threatening way. One of them asked to try it on and I knew this was the prelude to a robbery. I picked up the pace and speed-walked to my house.

I put the Michael Jackson jacket in my closet and never wore it outside the house again. Occasionally, I'd pull it down and dance around in my bedroom in it, but that was as far as I was willing to go.

On one of her visits from Ireland, my kooky aunt Sheila found out about it. I guess she and my mother were laughing about the story. She asked me to bring it into the kitchen. Sheila would have been in her early forties at the time. Usually swathed head-to-toe in sensible brown wool, she was not a fashion risk-taker that I could recall.

But she liked that jacket.

She put it on, spun round a couple of times. When I would have expected her to hand it back, she sat down at the kitchen table in it and recommenced a conversation with my mother. I was being dismissed.

A few hours later, she was still in it.

My mother came to me: "Can Sheila have the jacket?"

What I should have said was, "No" or, better yet, "How much is she willing to give me for it?"

Instead, I opened the door: "Why?"

"You never wear it. And she likes it. Why not give it to her?"

So, stupidly, I did.

I never did find out what she did with it, or, more to the point, what she did *in* it.

Did she wear it around Dublin, hoping to stumble into a back-alley dance competition? Did she wear it to work at the Ministry of Agriculture, where she was some sort of bureaucrat? Did she go out with friends and everyone would sit around pretending that Sheila didn't look like a visitor from the near future or, possibly, a German? Did she know how ridiculous she looked?

Or did she have so much confidence that she didn't care what people thought? Was she a better, stronger person than I was? I suspect she was. I like to think she wore that Michael Jackson jacket all over the place, and did not give a simple fuck about what anybody said.

Though it was an expensive, unmitigated disaster, the "Beat It" jacket got me thinking about clothes. I guilted my mother into taking me to Simpsons so that I could buy myself an outfit—grey pleated denim chinos, a grey patterned dress shirt (it would have been okay if I'd stopped there, but . . .) and a blue denim vest.

I looked like a gentleman cowboy with airs or the world's most effete shitkicker.

But a girl in my class, Kelley, looked over at me as I sat down on a Monday morning and said, "You look nice," and it was all worth it. Nobody else said anything or needed to. One kind mention was perfect.

This was the sort of noticing I was interested in—subtle and glancing.

By reputation, the best-dressed man in Western history was Beau Brummell, an early-nineteenth-century bon vivant who didn't do much aside from going out-of-doors looking classy. He's credited with establishing the modern uniform of the professional class—a sober suit and tie.

Brummell had many thoughts on what constituted proper sartorial comportment (in quotations that are so perfect, they were either made up or workshopped at many, many parties for the purpose).

"If John Bull [the average man] turns to look at you on the street, you are not well dressed, but either too stiff, too tight or too fashionable."

And:

"To be truly elegant, one should not be noticed."

I wonder what Brummell would have thought of the "Beat It" jacket. I imagine he might have summoned a mob to beat the wearer—an obvious witch—to death.

Brummell is also given credit for establishing the coat as the core element in a man's wardrobe. As long as you had a well-cut coat of fine material, the rest of your outfit was inconsequential. The coat told people what you were about.

I can chart my life through coats.

After the "Beat It" jacket, the next one that mattered was a trench coat. It was the first thing I'd ever owned that you could say was well tailored. I had seen it on Neil Tennant, the lead singer of the Pet Shop Boys, in the video for their first hit, "West End Girls." There is nothing to that video. It's mostly Tennant marching at the double-quick around London, trailed by the band's keyboardist. There is no choreography or story. What made the video iconic was Tennant's double-breasted full-length black trench coat. Per eighties style, the coat was too big on him, but other than that it's a timeless garment because everyone who puts one on immediately looks cooler.

I was fascinated by the way the coat swept around Tennant's ankles as he moved. Pop stars are often photographed in front of large fans. As the breeze catches their hair and clothing, it creates the illusion of movement and action. Tennant's trench coat captured that feeling. He looked like he was going somewhere.

The coat fit in with my changing presentation—all black, buckles, layers, pants pinned below the knee, weird Robert Smith hair. Though I had no friends who dressed that way, I was going full goth.

After a short while, it struck me that the look had something too effeminate about it. Too swirling and elaborate.

Also, the coat did you no favours in the Canadian climate—far too hot in the summer, not nearly warm enough in the winter. It is difficult to look steely when you are sweating like a pig that's been wrapped in black draping. The problem with a trench coat is that it's designed to be worn in a trench or the British Isles, where it's sopping wet all of the time. I have three or four of them now and I get to wear them about six weeks of the year. Eventually, I will hit a critical mass of trench coats and it will make good financial sense to move to London and starve there.

The next jacket iteration was my favourite—a bog-standard black leather biker jacket, the sort worn by real rock gods. I'd come back around to my first musical crush, Joan Jett.

Of the many things that you do not realize when you are young, the most frustrating is that this is your one chance at a great many things. Nobody reminds you of that. And when they do, you can't hear them.

You will never again be free of the obligation to work. You won't be able to sleep until noon (see under: work). You won't spend entire weekends at someone else's house doing nothing but watching TV. Your friendships will never again be so intense. There are dozens of things I would like to go back in time to tell my younger self. Not of the "Do this differently" variety (though there are those), but more along the lines of "Soak this up. This is happening now, and soon won't ever again."

The black leather biker jacket is one of those things. That's a lifetime one-off that you get a pass on from ages fifteen to twenty-one.

What do you think to yourself when you see a forty-year-old guy in a black leather biker jacket taking a toddler to buy ice cream, dressed up like Joey Ramone with male pattern baldness?

"He looks nice" or "I'll bet he's a good man to have backing you in a fight" or "I would like to spend a day making love to that rugged adventurer"?

No, you think only one thing: "How sad." And then you think another: "Is there no one who loves this man enough to tell him how sad he looks? He's got a kid. Where's his wife in this? She shares some of the blame. Or maybe they're divorced and this was part of her revenge. How wicked."

There is no going back to the leather biker jacket, not for men. Twenty-one is a hard stop.

A small exception can be made for working musical artists (defined as those who have cut studio albums in the last five years and can sell out a three-hundred-seat venue) until the age of thirty. But that's it. Even the Ramones started to look stupid after fifty.

Women get a biker jacket pass until whatever age, since they can wear one in an ironic, gender-bending, Le Smoking sort of way.

Men, there is no irony possible. Everyone knows what you're up to—you're reliving the glory days. That you feel so desperate a need to relive them suggests they weren't all that glorious. Which is another level of tragedy.

Certain jackets are meant for certain very specific times. If I missed out on dozens of the things that you can only do with dignity as a child—going to Disneyland, riding a skateboard, crying in public—at least I got that one right.

After the leather jacket, there was an Oakland Raiders parka.

I did not like the Raiders in any special way. At the time I only had room in my heart for Notre Dame football, but the Raiders jacket had a perfectly severe aesthetic. It was simple and black, with the team name stencilled across the back in block silver lettering. Also—a bonus—it was warm.

It was another jacket with a musical connection, having been popularized by Public Enemy. That group's military presentation (they had their own ersatz armed wing—Security of the First World) appealed to me. I was in the midst of reading *The*

Autobiography of Malcolm X and having a working-class-white-kid reaction to its message of radical self-exploration. I was trying to be more myself by copying other people. I didn't detect the irony. (Though I have to say that, all these years later, Malcolm X would rank in my best-dressed hall of fame.)

People at school liked that jacket. Too much, as it turned out. Word quickly got back to me in the broken-telephone style of high school that someone was looking to steal it. Who exactly? They couldn't say. Or the name changed. The threat was obscure. I got paranoid.

I couldn't leave the jacket in my locker, so for the better part of a year, I wore it everywhere. I couldn't lay it across the back of a chair in the lunchroom and go outside for a cigarette. It had to come with me.

As a result, that jacket and I became inextricably linked. It was a big school and many of the kids there didn't know me. I became "the guy with the Oakland Raiders jacket." I stopped wearing anything else. I wore that thing in spring and summer. My body adapted, modulating my internal environmental controls. I grew comfortable in it, like new skin, and I couldn't move on to whatever jacket was meant to come next. It wasn't something I wore anymore. It was me.

Then I went to a house party, had several drinks, forgot my rules, left it lying on a bed and it was stolen. I was bereft, but I could soon see the wisdom in it. I wasn't ever going to let that thing go. It had to be taken away for my own good. In the end, I wonder if it was one of my friends doing me a favour.

I thought I might switch back to the biker jacket, but the one I owned no longer fit right. I wanted the same thing again, only a bit bigger. Exactly the same thing.

At this point—aged seventeen—I no longer spoke to my father.

Very occasionally, he'd try to come to see me at school and be rebuffed at the office. He'd leave me long, ornate letters written in red ink. I didn't bother reading past the first few lines. I don't know what point he was trying to make, but I didn't care to hear it. Whatever it was, I was sure I'd heard it before.

At Christmas each year, he'd phone the house to ask my brother and me what gifts we wanted. Those calls were awful— the way my mother would spasm upon hearing that unexpected, unwanted voice from the past. The way she'd hand me the phone and say "It's Niall," never "It's your father."

These conversations didn't touch me. The only thing I felt for him anymore was a dull resentment. I thought of the annual gift-giving as evening the score.

He'd never get you the thing you asked for. Instead, he'd get something he thought you'd like. Since he didn't know us anymore, it was always wrong. But that last year, I wanted something very specific—a new leather biker jacket. I'd found the perfect one in a shop on Yonge Street. I told him what it was called, where to get it and how much it cost.

His sister brought the presents by our house. I didn't bother leaving mine under the tree and opened it straight off. Of course, it wasn't what I'd asked for. It was a black leather jacket, but a puffy, cinch-waisted one that looked as if it had been stitched together from torn pieces. In its guido-ish way, it was as farcical as the "Beat It" jacket. It was something my father would have worn. I didn't even try it on.

I waited until after Christmas to call him.

I was working in a movie theatre downtown. There was a

windowless office in the back. After the doors were locked and everyone else had gone home, I went in there and dialled his number. Once it began to ring, I turned off the lights and sat there in total darkness.

The conversation started out cordially. I thanked him. He asked if I liked it. I tried the "yes, but . . ." route. I wondered if he still had the receipt and could I get that from him. He tried to convince me that this was a better jacket than the one I wanted. I should just try it for a while. I'd like it.

I pushed back harder. The tone went from conciliatory to clipped. I'm not sure who started the fight. Me, probably. I was itching for one. I was enjoying the feeling of baiting him. In the midst of the screaming, he snapped. He began shrieking in rage. He cursed me, my mother and my brother. He made threats that I cannot bring myself to write down here.

He was insane—he'd been institutionalized when I was in the seventh grade—but this was the first time I realized just how sick he was. No person in their right mind could say these sorts of things. He had always been erratic—something much more than moody. He swung violently from up to down on the emotional meter without any warning. One minute going on about some bit of news he'd heard, the next minute ranting about some half-connected thought. You learned to approach him from the side, like a large animal, never quite letting him get a fix on you.

This all seems quite normal when you've never been used to anything else. It isn't discussed or rolled over in your mind. It's a simple reality to be handled as best you can.

When he was put in the mental hospital, it was presented to me in the same way that I might've been told he'd got a job in a foreign country or gone on a long vacation. Since my mother didn't make a big deal of it, I didn't either.

I'd go to see him once in a while. I recall sitting across from him on a stairwell landing that had a barred gate. We'd both pulled up chairs to either side. I wasn't allowed in with him, which I suppose should have struck me, but didn't.

It went on like that for weeks. And then he was out. We never discussed it, but that was after the debacle in North Bay and I wasn't seeing him much or at all. It was the beginning of our long drift apart.

Now, four years later, as I sat in the dark, he was finally revealing to me just how damaged he was.

It wasn't an epiphany. I didn't weep or sit there trembling half the night or any other sort of cinematic response. I knew it was the end, but it didn't feel like a milestone in my life. He'd been absent for so long in every meaningful way that I no longer felt he'd ever been there at all. So I didn't feel the loss of him. He was someone I once knew. That was all.

I hung up and went home. I never spoke to my father again. He died when I was nineteen.

HAIR

AFTER MY PARENTS DIVORCED, we briefly moved in with my mother's only brother, Michael, and his wife and kids. Like my mother, Michael was not an effusive person. I remember him as I do the rest of us—sitting around the kitchen table for hours at a time. We were like some renaissance Flemish painting of a burgher family—stuck forever in a scene of bland domesticity.

Michael was the first man I'd spent time around who was bald. Going back through the family albums, it was clear that Michael had started losing his hair in his twenties. By the time he had kids, he also had a monk's tonsure. He looked sixty when he was forty.

My father on the other hand had the hair of a badger. It spread over his head like shag carpeting. He could grow a decent beard in the space of a day. He had a moustache like the Kaiser.

After a while, it occurred to me that these two men represented the polarities of my hair possibilities. I was going to end up like one or the other.

Well, Jesus, Christ, what if I was headed in Michael's direction?

I went to my mother for the good word on this. Was I going to be bald?

My mother had the Irish way of saying things she wasn't at all sure of with enormous certainty. She wasn't lying or making stuff up, as such. She was telling you the thing she knew would get you off her neck. She was busy and so wasn't going to waste time on semantics. This tendency toward the easy way out was reassuring, but you had to take the Stalin route with her on many things—Trust, but check.

No, my mother said, you are not going to be bald. Michael was bald because he worked in construction.

Sorry, how's that?

According to my mother, concrete made you bald. Or rather, being in the vicinity of concrete in its powdered state caused people to lose their hair. The physics of this corrosive process were not explained.

On its face, this is ludicrous. Go to any construction site. It is not a collection of differently bodied Mr. Cleans. Women work construction. None of them are bald.

If concrete made you bald, they'd have figured out a way to make skyscrapers out of popsicle sticks.

But like most people do, I chose to believe the comforting lie. It became an article of faith. I talked about it a lot (i.e., I worked very hard to talk myself into something I knew in my bones was not true). I went so far as to convince many of my friends of the insidious secret of concrete. Avoid all building materials. That's what you have to do if you want to be your own Omar Sharif. If you're mindful of that, you have no need to worry.

For as long as I knew anything about hair, say from the age of seven or eight years old, I was possessed by it.

In summer, the sight of chest hair or underarm hair enthralled me. When would that happen to me? It was visual confirmation of maturity.

This fixation drove me beyond the bounds of decency. When I first spotted a small growth of pubic hair, I invited my mother to get a load of this, waistband of my underwear pulled out, stupidly proud. I was young, but not that young.

My mother jerked her head away and said, "That's fine. I don't need to see that."

I took for granted the hair on my head. It wasn't good hair. I knew that even then. Indeterminately brown, thin, lank, with a cowlick.

It hadn't been first cut until I was about four years old, so through most of my early childhood I looked like a feral member of The Beatles.

The Greeks in the neighbourhood repeatedly shaved the heads of their children in infancy—boys and girls—to promote growth and thickness. Obviously, this sort of foresight is why the Greeks invented democracy. We, on the other hand, waited timidly for the problems to land on us from a great height so that we could enjoy the pleasure of complaining about them.

My mother cut my hair for the first time with a pair of household shears. It was never right again.

After that, I got my hair cut up on Dundas Street by an old-timey Italian barber named Joe. It was always an occasion, because it was one of the few things I did with my father. My mother would not have been able to keep her peace with all the nudie magazines spread about the place.

Joe began each session with a long consult. What would I like him to do? How long? And the sides? Sure. What about style?

Then he'd cut my hair the way he liked it—a proto–Wall Street crewcut, parted severely to one side. For years, that was my hairstyle—The Joe. Every kid I knew had the same haircut, because most people I knew went to Joe. He was cheap, professional and did not obviously hate children, which was a more socially acceptable position in the eighties.

Once I got to high school, I got philosophical about my hair. What is it expressing about my inner self? When people see me, what are they thinking?

My hair aspirations changed with my musical tastes. I would have liked to have had long heavy metal hair. But my hair did not grow quickly, and the intermediate stage—shoulder length with curling, Farrah-Fawcettish bangs—made me look like a squirrel hunter from the Ozarks.

Many of the biggest new wave acts were then showcasing what might be called "The Exaggerated Elvis"—tight on the sides, bangs swept up off your forehead into a gelled wave that breaks toward the back of your head. The higher the better.

Some kids could get that front facade six inches or more over their hairline. But they had good hair.

I tried it for a while. I could just barely make it work at home. But by the time I got to school, my cowlick had assumed control. The front edge split and collapsed. The bangs fell over my face like drapery. I'd have been okay if The Happy Mondays had been a thing, but Britpop was still a few years off. I had that dull, mopey look before it was a rage. It's still no consolation.

By this time, I'd abandoned Joe. His charting of trends had been behind the times when I was eight and now that I was fourteen, it had become medieval.

Like most ambitious young men, I began to visit my mother's hairdresser. She got her hair done at a unisex salon in the basement of Simpsons department store downtown.

When you see a modern hair palace in the movies, it has the feel of a daytime nightclub. A thumping soundtrack, a lot of laughs and beautiful people, stylists leaned in over women's shoulders shrieking, "My God, you finally look like the real you!"

This wasn't that sort of place. It was small, dingy and overlit. Most of the customers in there were like my mother—hassled, middle-aged women who worked in nearby offices who needed to get in, get out and get home.

I'd meet my mother down at Simpsons every six or eight weeks after work. We'd both get our hair done by her lady, Kay. This was my way of getting out of paying. When we got to the register, I'd put my hands in my pockets and become fascinated by something off in the distance.

Kay was lovely, but workmanlike. She'd do what I asked, but I wasn't sure what to ask for. It never quite turned out.

One day, while waiting for Kay to finish up with my mother, I spotted him across the room—the man who would become my spiritual advisor, Mike.

Not all the important moments of recognition in your life are romantic. Or, not in the way you think. I had never seen anyone who looked like Mike. At least, I'd never seen anyone who looked that way *at work*.

He was in his twenties. He was wearing Lycra tights, half-laced combat boots and a v-neck t-shirt that he'd cut at the neck so that it billowed open nearly to his belly button. The entire ensemble was black. He had make-up on—eyeliner and maybe a hint of lip gloss.

And his hair. He'd shaved it to stubble up the back and sides. What remained on top was pushed over his face in an asymmetric arrow that slashed at forty-five degrees toward one corner of his chin. You could see only one eye when you looked at him.

This was what I wanted. I wanted to be this guy.

Not exactly, of course. Some of the elements of this look were a bit too ambitious for me.

Mike was also the first bodybuilder I'd ever known, an enormously muscled man.

Nowadays I would say of him, "Only a man that fit could get away with wearing yoga pants out of the house." Back then I thought, "Only a man that muscly could leave the house in spandex and not get the shit beaten out of him."

Here was someone who was his own man and who did not care. He was Joan Jett in real life. He stood out. I wanted that.

I asked at the desk if he had any openings. My mother finished up. I explained what I was doing. She looked over at Mike, shrugged and left. She did not leave any money. My freeloading days had ended.

I expected Mike to be haughty and aloof. He was not. He was bright and chatty. For a man so large, he had a nervous, twitchy way. He was excited by the idea that I'd asked for him. That's what he said—"excited." He asked me what I wanted. I didn't know what to say. "Something cool." Mike tidied my Exaggerated Elvis into a more manageable shape.

He said that before the next time I came in, I should think about what I wanted. Bring a picture. He shook my hand and said that it had been great to meet me. I swooned.

I went out and spent a bundle on imported British music magazines. I found what I needed in there—a moody black-and-white portrait of Robert Smith. Smith was the lead singer of The Cure, one of my favourite bands. He'd combined the ghoulishness of horror punk, the garishness of glam metal, and the loopy stage aesthetics of prog rock and subverted them all by producing irresistible, factory-style pop. Like all the rock stars I most admired, he projected the air of a man who did not care what you thought of him. He was going to do what he liked.

I was never going to be Morrissey—waifish, cut flowers in my back pocket, hair swept up four feet off my head. I didn't have the body. Any part of it. I could be Smith—dour, lumpy and unimpressed by the world. That wouldn't be much of a stretch

Though none of my friends dressed this way, I'd begun slowly morphing into him. I'd bought a pair of buckled, rubber-soled creepers. I'd begun rolling my pants around my legs below the knee and pinning them there. I was phasing all colour out of my wardrobe. Everything new that I bought was black.

But being Smith was not a function of fashion. It was the hair.

Smith swept his up off his head in a messy, skyward tangle. It wasn't a style, so-called. His hair just went up where it should be going down.

I went back to Mike—this time he was wearing a poncho and I made a mental note—"Buy poncho"—and showed him the picture. Then we had a heart-to-heart.

"This is a big change," Mike said. "Are you sure about this?"

"Do you think it's the right thing to do?"

"I think you should do what you want to do."

"Will I look stupid?"

"No. You'll look different. Most cool people are different."

How do I remember that dialogue at a distance of thirty years? Because it was the first and only father–son chat I'd ever had.

I went home imagining the scene this new look would create—horror, tears, recriminations. I was coming in hot, like something out of the *Road Warrior*.

I wheeled in the door. My mother was in the kitchen. She stepped away from the counter so that she could get a good look at me.

And then she said, "It suits you."

That took a lot of the juice out of it.

To my disappointment, most of my peers accepted the hair on its own terms. There were a few comments, but after a couple of days at school, it was a new commonplace. I wanted to provoke a reaction and, in that very teenager-y way, no one wanted to give me what I wanted.

Then the work began.

The hair as initially cut was modest in its aspirations. Maybe three inches high. I'd shaved the back and sides. There wasn't too much of it and it was still relatively easy to sculpt with gel. As it grew, gel stopped working. I moved to hairspray, and a lot of it. After a few months, it was a true Smith-esque mop, which required real industry.

This was my morning ritual.

I wouldn't wash my hair. Once I did that, it took hours to tease back up to attention. My hair went weeks without coming into contact with water.

This was made easier in my house because our single bathroom was not equipped with a shower. At fourteen/fifteen, looking like the coat-check attendant in a sex dungeon, I still took baths each morning. There was never time to run and rerun separate tubs for each of us. The first person up got the fresh water. Which meant I was always lolling around in my brother's filth.

The hair had flattened overnight and required extensive sprucing up. The only product I could now find that was equal to the job was a hairspray called French Formula—Hard to Hold.

There were other, more extreme options. Egg whites and sugar were popular with the punk set, but I could never get the proportions right. And after an hour, my head began to smell like a rotting dog carcass.

Modelling glue was another thing I'd heard about. It was used mostly on mohawks. But if you screwed that up in the initial application, the only way to undo the damage was to shave your head. I couldn't take that risk.

French Formula was the most extreme tool that had still passed through a manufacturing process. It couldn't be bad for you. It's not like it was concrete or anything.

Most hairsprays give you a little shape and body. This stuff was plumbers' glue. It didn't come out of the aerosol can in a liquid mist. It shot out like silly string—already congealing upon contact with air. What it touched, it hardened into sculpture. I'd go at my head with the French Formula for five minutes or so, bent at the waist, letting gravity do the work. I went through a bottle a week. I couldn't fluff it out because once you got your fingers in there, they weren't coming back.

A girlfriend once reached up from behind and tried to caress my hair. She was a little too enthusiastic in her thrust and her hand got stuck in at the roots. There were several frantic minutes of struggle before I could get her disentangled without letting half my scalp go with her.

That hair got bigger. At its longest, it stood a good fifteen inches off the top of my head. Over the course of a day, the French Formula lost its efficacy and the structure began to droop over the sides. (This was a small moment in time in which holding up huge hair had become so epidemic at my high school that aerosol products were banned in the halls. The air was turning toxic.)

I developed an involuntary tic that involved lifting both hands to the sides and smoothing the hair upward until it regained shape. That was my thinking pose. Fondling the poodle on top of my head.

From a distance, it must have appeared that I was wearing a large, black mushroom cap as a hat. I looked idiotic.

Which I suppose was the point. I enjoyed the stares on the subway. I looked cartoonish now—all-black ensembles, leather biker jacket, hair pulled down over my eyes. I liked the way adults shrank from me. Being outside the herd made me feel special.

The hair did present practical problems. I had a job at a fast-food restaurant for part of this time and I had to net it during work hours. One morning, I was prepping a batch of french fries in a large oil cooker. The considerable heat it gave off was being sucked up into a ceiling duct by an industrial fan. I was half-asleep, my mind drifting, my body leaning, my hair jutting. One of my colleagues came into the back, yelped, picked a filthy cloth off a counter and began beating me with it. My hair had caught fire. A great deal of it went up that day.

After a while, it wasn't shocking enough. I needed new tweaks. Mike began shaving lines in the back and around the side—straight ones at first. Then Charlie Brown zigzags. When I asked him to shave words, he demurred. He was only charging twenty-five bucks and didn't have that kind of time.

It's more likely he was trying to save me the embarrassment of taking a step too far. I was headed toward a safety pin through the nose.

Then one day, I called to make an appointment and they told me Mike had left.

We had not had personal conversations. We talked about bands and clothes and bars. These were practical sessions—I used him as a lifestyle guide and personality crutch. As long as Mike, this evidently cool person, thought I was cool, then I was.

He seemed to get a kick out of this strange mentoring role, an hour or so of it every two months for a couple of years. Big Brothers for goths.

But he had this same light relationship with all of his clients. I'd seen many old ladies squirming delightedly in his chair as he teased or flattered them. He wasn't a person who made distinctions. I was one of many. I didn't even know his last name.

In the post-Mike grief stages, I had my hair shaved briefly into a mohawk, but that was even more work. When you see mohawks in popular culture, they are standing up. That is a lie. Mohawks tilt. That's what they do.

So I chopped off my hair and went back to being a square. I shed some things (the buckle boots, the pants pinning) and kept others (the leather jacket, the sneer).

Of course—of course, of course, of course—I started to go bald in my late twenties. Genetics are to blame (and possibly concrete), but I still suspect French Formula.

I was lucky in my timing. By the early aughties, the greatest hero of all bald men—Michael Jordan—had made a shaved head fashionable. I had the misfortune of seeing a photograph of myself taken from above and behind. I was twenty-nine. I wasn't bald, but I was headed in that direction in a hurry. That same day, I had my head shaved.

I haven't had a barber of any description for fifteen years. I'm back to home care.

Once, when I was away for work for six weeks, I decided to grow it out and see what was left. I thought, "Maybe it's not that bad. Maybe if you give it a little length off the back it'll look cool in that British aristo, Michael Gambon in 'Layer Cake' way."

It's that bad. And, no, that won't work.

If I live to a decent age, hair will have been only a small part of my life. It's a reminder—make sure to enjoy childish things while you are a child. I like to think I did that part right.

THE SUBWAY

THE ONLY PERSON IN MY FAMILY who could drive was my father. He wasn't very good at it.

Around the time I was four or five, he went on permanent disability and dedicated his waking hours to drinking. If you were going to get into a vehicle with him, it was advisable to do so in the morning.

On one of those early shopping trips, he pulled his pickup out of a parking lot and turned directly into oncoming traffic. There was a low-speed head-on collision. I was sitting in the front seat thinking that this was all quite exciting. The police came and everything.

The parking lot was in front of the liquor store. He'd been in there buying a couple of forties of Captain Morgan. I'm not sure how he talked his way out of that one, but he had a knack for escaping.

After my parents split up, my father downgraded to a decrepit Volkswagen Rabbit. It was so rusted out, there was a hole the size of a dinner plate in the driver's side wheel well. This was literally a Flintstone car. You could push it with your feet.

He told me he'd bought it because it was good on gas. The starter went wonky. Rather than get the car fixed, my father's solution to this problem was to shut the car off as rarely as possible. During the day, he'd leave it in his garage running. When he needed to go somewhere, he'd run out, cover his mouth, lift the door, wait for the cloud of carbon dioxide to drift off toxically into the neighbourhood and then head out.

He had a plan for the car. He was going to wreck it and get the Blue Book value from insurance. That was real money. He couldn't just run it into a wall, of course. That would be suspicious. I still remember the Blue Book value—three thousand dollars. My father would say it a lot, hitting a high note on the second syllable—"three THOUsand dollars."

Alongside drinking and using his home as a rooming house for oddballs and degenerates, pursuing this idea had become his job. I never did tell my mother about it. There didn't seem much point.

The best way he could think to get away with his auto-destruct caper was to lure someone at a red light into a drag race. He'd get out ahead, slam on the brakes and the following car would catastrophically rear-end the Rabbit. With him in it. And possibly me.

In fairness, the seatbelts worked fine.

He tried this many times. Stop at the light. Significant look over at the guy alongside him. Total confusion on that guy's part ("Why is this man staring at me?"). Theatrical revving of the engine. Anxious, false bursts toward the line. And then the launch when the light turned. Either the other guy didn't take him up on it or the other car was so much more powerful than the pathetic Rabbit that it sped off ahead of us.

Of course, I knew it was a gigantically stupid idea, but there was no arguing with him when he was in that car. I'd once tried—some pointless digression about politics—and he'd become so angry that he'd pulled over to the side of the highway and told me to get out. Then he drove off. The highway cut through downtown a half-hour from where I lived. I climbed over the guard railing, skittered down an embankment and walked home. I was eleven years old and it had long before occurred to me that my father wasn't quite right in the head.

Every friend of mine was obsessed with the idea of hitting sixteen and getting a car. But cars made me anxious. Every time I got in one, it was *Death Race* with absurdly low stakes. My mother had never learned to drive. We couldn't have afforded a car in any case. There wasn't any real need of one and I didn't feel its loss. I had the subway.

The subway gets a bad rap because it is seen as a conveyance of need rather than desire. But I thought of it rather the other way around. You went to certain designated spots and professionals—people who didn't want to crash their vehicles for the insurance money—were on hand to take you to your destination. A transit system is chauffeuring for the masses.

The subway is predictable. It comes by every few minutes. It goes to the same places in the same order every time. Even children can figure it out. It is consistent.

You could stand at the front of the train, look out the window and feel its speed. When it got hot in summer, the driver left his door open and you could watch him turn the big lever. The subway was all my fantasies about motion, dependability and power come to life.

When I was nine, my friend Aaron and I began going downtown on Saturdays to the Eaton Centre, a large, ugly mall. There was nothing in the Eaton Centre for us. We had no money, and no idea how to spend it if we had. We went so that we could take the subway. Once there, we hung around until it made sense to go back.

On one occasion, a security guard stopped us while we were stealing coins from a fountain.

"Where are your parents?"

"Home."

"Why aren't you with them?"

"We wanted to take the train."

"Well, you can't be here."

Which was fine with us. All he was doing was telling us to get back on the subway. Which was the goal.

I went home and told my mother about it.

"I think he was worried that someone would kidnap us."

My mother nodded.

"Are you worried that someone would kidnap us?"

"Why would someone kidnap you?"

"For money, maybe?"

"You see any money around here?"

She had this way of turning things around until they made sense. Or, at least, made sense in a way you hadn't considered.

Sometimes Aaron and I would take the subway out to its final stop and sit in the station awhile. No one lived out there (or so it seemed). It was quiet. We didn't talk a whole lot. We liked to sit there, assessing the distances we'd crossed. And then we'd get back on the train. It was a pointless way to spend the day, but I suppose we could've been up to much worse. We'd get there soon enough.

In high school, we used the subway as a twisted playground. It was the place you went for that hour after school when nothing good happens. Each of us kept a collection of nickels that had been flattened by passing trains. In retrospect, the only reason we did this was to enjoy the thrill of watching people lose their minds as we jumped down onto the tracks to place and retrieve the coins. The souvenirs produced were useless. One looked exactly like any other, all its nickelly features flattened into a silver disc half as thick and twice as wide. I had dozens of them.

We played a game of chicken that involved "riding" the trains out of the station. As the doors closed and after the conductor had stopped paying attention, we'd step from the platform into the indentation of the doorway and brace ourselves against the sides. The idea was to hang on to the exterior of the train for as long as possible without being crushed by the barrier at the end of the platform.

Obviously, this was an unbelievably stupid thing to do. Most of us—including me—couldn't make it more than a few feet without panicking. As we sprang from the doorway, we'd occasionally glance off a pillar or into a wall. The floors were slick marble and we'd end up taking a humiliating fall, hammering into a bench or garbage can on the way down. We all agreed it was great fun and then limped off home to moan in our rooms.

It was performative masochism. Whom exactly we were performing it for was never clear. For a while there, jumping off things became a sort of mania for us—garages, fences, walls. Anything we could get on top of. We should have died many times over, but it never ended in anything worse than a turned ankle or chipped tooth.

I watched a guy leap out of a window in grade eleven math class. He'd been in an argument with the teacher and, in order to bring his point home with the proper dramatic flourish, he got up on the sill and announced that he was going to jump.

"So do it," the teacher said.

And he did.

It was at least two storeys down. Twenty-five feet minimum. I didn't see him land. I only saw the aftermath. He'd hit a wall splay-legged on the way down and shattered his tailbone. He lay there on the grass shrieking while the teacher had what looked to my inexpert eye something like the opening stages of a nervous breakdown.

One afternoon, a friend named Peter took train riding further than any of us ever had. He hopped onto the last car and rode it the full length of the platform. For a horrible moment, it seemed as if he might ride it right into the tunnel. The idea that anybody might be able to get by the barrier—a low steel gate—had not occurred to us. We were watching the clouds part and a miracle in the offing. My God, what a legend Peter would have been if he'd managed that.

Far too late, Peter thought better of the idea. With perhaps forty or fifty feet of platform remaining and the train now moving close to full speed, he leapt from the doorway.

I understood inertia in theory, but the true awfulness of Newtonian physics did not become apparent to me until this moment. Peter came cartwheeling off the train, arms akimbo, legs flailing. We could only see his back, but we all felt his despair. There was something sad and resigned in his spastic movements.

He broke into an exaggerated, involuntary sprint. He was

Wile E. Coyote going over the cliff's edge. Then he hit the wall at the end of the platform face first and bounced off it like India rubber. There was a lot of blood.

The rest of us waited to see if he was still twitching. When he began pathetically rising to his feet—nose broken, almost certainly concussed—everyone laughed. Hard. Even Peter.

Later, Peter robbed a drug store by kicking a hole in a long, vertical plate-glass window and crawling in underneath it. He wanted cigarettes. While he was on the way back out, what remained of the window dislodged and a shard of glass gouged a horrific hunk of skin and hair from his skull.

Rather than call it an evening, Peter went on to the house party we were all attending. When the cops broke it up, they couldn't help but notice the kid whose head was bleeding profusely through his hoodie. One of the brighter bulbs on the force then recalled the piece of scalp they'd recovered at a robbery earlier in the night.

Peter was arrested and housed temporarily in a juvenile unit. He was the sort of person who had a supernatural ability to get on your nerves, like a werewolf of irritation. He managed his trick again in the wrong place and one of the other pipsqueak convicts stabbed him right through the hand with a pencil. Peter returned incredibly proud of this numbskull stigmata. He'd show the hole to anybody who asked.

I could not tell you now very much about the lives of most of my work colleagues. Where do they live, who with and what do their parents do for a living? I have no idea. But in high school, I knew those things about dozens of classmates. I knew where they worked and who they were seeing and the model of car they drove.

The ones I kept closest track of were the achievers. They were doing things and going places.

My best friends were not achievers. They were cheerful nitwits and scholastic failures. They didn't expect to get anywhere and we never spoke of the future. It did not interest us in the least. We were creatures entirely of the present. What could be done today? That was the focus.

Without achievements, we instead took our pride from endurance. We could get through things. Pain was a big part of that. Hurting ourselves for others to see. We liked to play another variant of chicken, with cigarettes.

Two guys press their forearms together, and then drop a lit cigarette in between. You don't feel much at first. You smell it before you feel it—hair burning, flesh melting. And then you really feel it. You lose by pulling your arm away, allowing the cigarette to fall to the ground.

I still have those scars. I can go up and down my body cataloguing all the other marks left by the recklessness of childhood— the time I accidentally hit myself with an axe, the groove left after John dropped a stereo speaker on me, the spot on my neck where a sliver of metal flecked off a bar as someone was hitting me in the head with it. There's a chance I'm slowly dying of lead poisoning as I write this.

I once woke up and found what I thought was a thick, black hair sticking out of my forehead. Instead, it was stitching thread that had worked its way to the surface over time. I couldn't remember when I'd had it stitched. There was a lot of stitching at the time.

Enduring was the key, and the subway was symbolic of that for me.

I did not expect that I would ever get the chance to go to interesting places or see new things. If you'd asked one of us about backpacking through Europe or whatever it is that people with money do when they are on the cusp of adulthood, we'd have laughed at you. Yeah, give us that money. We'll buy a hundred two-fours and have the most epic summer in history without ever having to leave John's or Brian's or Ned's garage. Europe. Go fuck yourself with Europe.

What I hoped for my life was that it would stay essentially the same. I craved orderliness and stability. Like my father, I had a dollar figure in mind—forty thousand.

If I could find a job that paid me forty grand, I could have all the things I wanted. I wouldn't fear disruption or disaster. I wanted to know that when I left in the morning, there would be something to come back to at night. Forty thousand would settle that for me.

On that pay packet, I'd never be able to afford my own car. It didn't matter. I couldn't drive and felt no need to learn.

Eventually, my mother got her driver's licence and bought a car—a little VW. I noted that she waited until I was out of the house to do it. So, in revenge, I got my driver's permit as well and decided I would be borrowing it often.

On one of those first trips, I rear-ended someone. My mother then forbade me the car. So I went back to the subway.

I know every stop by heart. I know who lived within walking distance of what station—Brian just up from Keele, Ned a few blocks from High Park, Ronan ten stops on the Runnymede bus.

I still live in the city. I own a nice car. I bought it because it scoops—a 305-horsepower turbo-charged engine. If I'd owned it as a teenager, it would have been a very expensive coffin.

I rarely drive it, because I still prefer taking the subway. Unlike everything else about my life, and in particular my expectations, it has not changed.

DUNGEONS & DRAGONS

IN THE MID TO LATE EIGHTIES, no hobby marked you as a sexually deficient weirdo with no hope in life quite as much as Dungeons & Dragons. Every one of the dozens of books you needed to figure the game out should have been subtitled "Losing at Everything: A Guide."

My contemporaries were arranged into three broad swaths—the people who played Dungeons & Dragons; the people who secretly played Dungeons & Dragons; and the people who had heard of Dungeons & Dragons but did not play it because they knew people who played Dungeons & Dragons and didn't want to end up that way.

I was in a subset of the second category. I didn't *play* Dungeons & Dragons. That wouldn't happen until much later, and only the once. But I knew everything about it and told no one that I did.

I got interested in the game—if that's the right word for something as Byzantine and immersive as D&D (don't laugh at me)—when I was helping my friends buy modelling glue.

By age fifteen, many of my friends were jaded drug users. They'd smoked all the weed, dropped all the acid and were looking for new flavours of escapism. None of us knew how to get hold of heroin or cocaine, or could afford it if we had. Crack wasn't a thing yet. There were no designer drugs, or none that we'd ever heard of.

Then one of my friends heard about glue. It was cheap, easy and got you stupidly high.

I watched my buddy Adam do it once. He took a tube of modelling glue, the sort that is used to put together miniature replica airplanes or attach tin soldiers to an ersatz battlefield. He squeezed the glue into a plastic bag, held the bag to his face and breathed in and out. We called it "huffing."

Some things are ugly and some things look that way. Huffing glue is both. From the first inhalation, Adam's eyes started rolling around and he began listing to one side. The smell was metallic and repulsive. After a few minutes, he dropped the bag and his hands fell slowly into his lap in a bizarrely simian gesture, palms up. He wasn't aware of me anymore. Or of anything really. He was staring at a point over my shoulder, looking confused. He'd lost control.

There was a wet crust around his lips that quickly hardened—"gluebeard."

Adam was a handsome kid in the all-American sense—tall, broad, blond. After thirty seconds on the bag, he looked like he'd been run through a car wash on a bicycle. Glue huffing had a way of immediately making everyone who did it dishevelled.

I was not a drug person. This wasn't moralism. I just could never get my head around the whole idea.

First off, drugs are done in furtive groups. Five guys roll a joint. One of them puts it in his mouth, which is a petri dish of disease and contagion. Then he gives it to another guy. *Who also puts it in his mouth.* And then another mouth. And another. Eventually, back to the original mouth.

The second problem with drugs is that someone is always trying to rip you off as you buy them. We didn't have regular dealers. We had places to go where dealers tended to congregate. They were all faceless and nameless to us, since we wanted to be that same way to them.

One of those spots was in a laneway in behind Lansdowne subway station. You could get all sorts there. Most of it was overpriced and underpowered, but we enjoyed the feeling of buying drugs—all the nodding, stage-whispering and palming of bills and packages. It was the closest we were ever going to get to spycraft.

At least one time out of three, whatever we'd bought turned out not to be what had been promised.

That's why I preferred liquor—it's a state-run industry. It has standards.

Also, drugs—all of them—made me ill. I suspect that's largely because I could only overcome my squeamishness when I was already blind drunk.

I was convinced to give hash one last sober try after our friend Isaac found a real and permanent drug connect—a guy he worked with on weekends at an auto-repair shop.

We smoked the hash on the football field of our high school. Since this was all for science, I went at it hard. It hit me like a sandbag coming out of the rafters. I had been very drunk and pretty high, but I had never felt anything like this. I couldn't speak. I had no sense of space or time. I could not stand up or bear to lie down. I was hallucinating all sorts of nonsense, while being dimly aware that I was hallucinating it.

John quite literally dragged me to his house, which was just up the street. His room was in the basement. He put me down on his waterbed. The undulating did not help. He turned on music to soothe me—"Money" by Pink Floyd. The roll-in with cash registers opening and coins jingling would not stop and the song would not start. When I tried to turn off the stereo, "off" and "on" would switch places. No matter which way I turned it, I was turning it on. Clearly, I was going mad.

I staggered upstairs to announce my impending lunacy to John and was confronted instead by his mother. In my panic to escape her, I turned back and went headfirst down a flight of stairs. Apparently, the hash had given me superhuman suppleness, because I didn't snap my neck. John's mother was still standing at the top of the basement stairs while he tried to talk her down—"It's totally fine. I think he's just not feeling great." I found my way into the furnace room, turned off the lights and passed out on the floor.

The next day, I was as sick as I'd ever been. I felt very close to paralyzed. The hangover, if that's what you'd call it, lasted nearly a week.

Of course, hash isn't supposed to do this to you. Isaac went back and asked his new drug-dealing pal if we'd been given an especially narcotic batch. Apparently, as a "little surprise," he had given us some laced with opium.

So there's the last and most important reason why I didn't do drugs—little surprises. Nobody puts powerful psychotropics in gin. The gin does that work for you.

My abstemiousness, however, was not widely shared in my peer group. Hence the glue.

Modelling glue was reasonably priced. The problem was acquisition. You can only buy it in hobby stores and there was only one of those in our neighbourhood. You also need a certain kind of plastic baggie to do it, since shopping bags leak and sandwich bags are too small.

In an age before the ubiquity of Ziploc, the correct baggies were also sold at the hobby store. And once you've done some glue, you need more glue. Immediately. You can never have enough glue.

Let's role-play this. If Adam wants glue, he goes to the hobby store to get some. Say, three tubes and ten baggies. It was a big place and fairly busy. Easy enough to blend in. The guy behind the counter sees Adam and thinks, "I wonder what he's building?"

It may strike him as odd that Adam is buying glue but shows no interest in the model kits. But whatever. It's a free country.

It strikes him as a little more odd when Adam comes in the next day to buy more glue and more baggies. By the third day, this guy behind the counter has it figured out. Now it's like buying a ski mask at a gun store. Once you're cut off at the hobby shop, that's the end of your glue because there was no glue dealer lurking behind Lansdowne station.

Even my idiot friends could see this problem coming. No one person could buy glue repeatedly. Different people would have to buy it at different times. The baggies would have to be part of a separate purchase. I was not interested in doing glue, but I try to be helpful. So I became the guy who got the baggies.

Now you're not just going to wheel in and buy a box of baggies on the regular. That's also weird. You have to spend some time in there making it seem like baggies are something you remembered to get as you were leaving.

At fourteen, I had passed beyond comic books and models didn't do it for me. What they had in the hobby store that piqued my interest was a vast collection of Dungeons & Dragons paraphernalia.

I'm going to suppose that you know the fundamentals. It's the most basic sort of narrative—a man goes on a journey. Except it's not necessarily a man. It's a dwarf or an elf or a half-elf Druid or a part-dwarf sorcerer or some other bizarre mélange of imaginary ethnicity. You are that dwarf. You build him from the ground up. You're supposed to do this with the randomness of rolled dice to avoid making him the smartest, most muscular dwarf in all of dwarfdom. Then you and a few friends begin a merry adventure through the Land of Fallen Men or whatever, killing things and finding treasure as you go.

In order to understand the limitations and possibilities of your dwarf doppelganger, you require Dungeons & Dragons manuals. A lot of them. Dungeons & Dragons created the wiki model before such a thing existed on the internet. The information was voluminous and crowd-sourced. It was always expanding further into the minutiae of armour, weapons or spell casting. You were always behind the latest developments and needed another book to catch up.

And these books were not cheap. What could have been shoehorned into a mass market paperback would instead be bound in glossy hardcover volumes that were twenty, thirty bucks a pop. I made $3.15 an hour sweating over a deep fryer at Harvey's. I'd work a whole shift to buy one book.

But the vastness of it, the detail, the way the information had been broken into lists and catalogues and instructionals, was irresistible to me. This was a unique system of thought so capacious you knew you could never fully grasp it.

I WAS HAPPY TO GET THE BAGGIES for my friends, but I wasn't going to do it for free. We had a round-up understanding. You gave me a bill and I gave you no change. I used the first few turns at this to seed my Dungeons & Dragons project.

My friends—Adam, Tony, Geoff—were quickly turning into full-on degenerates. Glue is awfully hard on the body. It sticks to your lungs and accumulates. It kills millions of brain cells per inhalation. Brain cells do not regenerate.

I had lunch with Adam one day at a restaurant off school grounds. He wasn't looking too good, nubby and worn down. Like a human pencil eraser. I wondered how often he did glue now. Every day? Several times every day? My friends knew I found the whole thing sordid and began to hide it from me. They'd stopped expecting me to buy the baggies. I didn't ask where they were getting them now.

During lunch, Adam began hacking. It was loud and consistent enough that people turned to see if he was all right. After a few minutes at it, he coughed something up. It was a piece of hardened glue a little bit smaller than a marble.

I was reckless in the same way most of my friends were, but I wasn't willfully self-destructive. I wasn't going to ruin myself just for the sake of doing so. The people I admired lived hard, but they got up the next morning. They went to school and had jobs afterward. They fulfilled their responsibilities. As stupid as I was, I recognized where that line fell and was not going to cross it. Coughing up glue in a greasy spoon on Dundas Avenue West at noon on a Tuesday. This wasn't rock 'n' roll.

Something in my lizard brain was telling me, "This won't end well. Flee." Unlike my actual brain, my lizard brain has rarely let me down. The glue period and the people involved faded from my life. When you are a teenager you think your friends will be intertwined in your daily drama forever. Those connections have an electric urgency. You need to constantly know what those people are doing and why and be part of it. But at a certain point, they begin to drop off. For all sorts of reasons, you stop caring. New people appear, that same connection is achieved, the urgency repeats (though it is less intense each time) and then it too passes.

Another marker of the arrival of adulthood is the realization that the only person who remains entirely consistent in your life is yourself, or some version of yourself. If you cannot find a way to be comfortable with that, you will struggle. Dungeons & Dragons became a way further into that fresh realization.

I had by now a critical mass of books. All the information was at hand. I would spend hours alone in my room, headphones on, making up characters and worlds. I filled hundreds of foolscap pages with notes and illustrations. I didn't think I was "playing" correctly. It was hard to say, since I didn't know how anyone else did it and I didn't care to ask. I didn't use dice or strictly adhere to the rules. I used the books as a leaping-off point. What I came up with was a step further than the established order of the books. It was my own.

I don't remember any of those characters because there were so many. Once I'd finished one to my liking (the point at which anyone else would have begun "playing"), I started another. They all had elaborate back stories. It was the act of creation that enthralled me.

I didn't write as a child. There is no corpus of handwritten short stories or angsty poems buried in my mother's basement. I stuck to writing whatever was assigned in school.

Instead, I taught myself to write by reading. The best way to uncover your own literary voice is to read widely enough that you find five or fifty authors whose style you deeply admire. Then copy them. Nothing I've ever written is half as good as the stuff I'm trying to emulate. But I do get paid. I get up every morning and do the work. It's something.

That's what I did with Dungeons & Dragons. I was copying what was in the books but reflecting it askance, in my own way. I did it rigorously. It cost me no effort (the best indicator that you're meant to do whatever you're doing). I could disappear into it for entire days.

My mother saw me at it often. Obviously, she thought the whole thing sad and bizarre. But she knew it was better than whatever the Adams and Tonys of the world were doing in their downtime. She never commented on my interest in goblins.

Eventually, I realized I was going to have to play the game, if only to wrap my arms around the entirety of it.

I tried to interest some other friends—my newer, better friends—to do it with me. I hadn't yet finished handing out all the materials on a Friday evening in John's basement when someone said, "What the fuck is an orc?" and the whole thing collapsed into jeers.

I joined a Dungeons & Dragons club. This cost me some pride. I was not a joiner and did not care to be told what to do. But it was the only logical step.

I lasted one day. The people in the club were adults but were clearly stunted in some way. Socially awkward, bad clothes, odd bodied, uniformly male, speaking in a weird D&D code.

Less than an hour in, I knew I'd made a terrible mistake. I kept doing things wrong, or jumping ahead, or interrupting. They kept telling me where I'd misinterpreted the texts or misunderstood them. This was church for dorks.

And the game itself was boring. Super boring. Outrageously boring. All you did was roll dice and listen to someone—the Dungeon Master—explain what had happened as a result. He wasn't very good at it. Not a natural storyteller. There was a lot of arguing. Even with all these rules, no one could agree on how exactly they were to be put into action.

My character was killed off early in the outing. And that was it.

I said I was going to the bathroom and walked out.

Just like that, the fixation dissipated. I stopped rereading the Dungeons & Dragons guidebooks. After a time, they were buried on a shelf in my room under other, better books. In the end, that was the point.

MUSIC

AT THE OUTSET of the grade four school year, we performed an experiment in taste. Each of us was given a questionnaire and asked to list the things we liked. Favourite food, favourite colour and so on.

"Favourite song" stopped me dead.

I didn't have a favourite song. Worse than that, I could not recall any song in particular. Now that my father was gone, there was no music in our house.

We no longer owned a stereo. We didn't listen to Top 40 radio. Nobody played an instrument. You hear stories about musical families. We were the amusical type. All our workaday suffering was done the way it should be—in silence.

Nonetheless, I had to come up with something here. What sort of loser doesn't know a single song? After a great deal of mental effort, I fetched one out of my memory: "The Battle of New Orleans" by Johnny Horton. (It's at this point that I encourage the reader to dial this tune up on YouTube. Put it on loud. Do it at work. Your colleagues will admire your iconoclasm.)

As songs go, this is a poor, verging on psychopathic, choice for a nine-year-old boy.

"The Battle of New Orleans" is the sort of song they'd play at a Civil War re-enactment or a Klan rally. It's the theme song of someone who is radically out of touch with modern life. This was not lost on me.

As an added humiliation, the teacher randomly selected students to explain some of their choices and sing their songs. Imagine that going as badly as it could possibly go—me, standing there, thinking about wetting my pants, while trying an early experiment in freestyle rap that went something like "We fired our guns and the British kept a comin', down the Mississippi to the Gulf of Mexico."

Nobody laughed. There is something worse than being laughed at. There is pity. And there is no worse pity than that of children. Since casual cruelty is one of their defining features, hitting the pity bar of a room of nine-year-olds is like reaching the stratosphere unaided by rocket boosters. Once you're there, you die from lack of oxygen.

After that humiliation, music became a mission. I was going to be musical. I was going to listen to music that other people enjoyed and learn to enjoy it myself. Being musical was a state of mind, and I would achieve that.

I began fiddling with the dial on the small radio in our kitchen. Until that point, it was set permanently to the local CBC station, where there was no music.

Now it was time to reach out into a wider world that did not include traffic accidents and policy updates and find *art*. Whatever that was. The first song that struck and stuck with me was Joan

Jett's remake of "I Love Rock 'n' Roll." That sounded propulsive and heavy.

I needed to find a picture of this Joan Jett to see if she looked right. A reconnoitre down at Mike's Smokes turned up a magazine with Jett on the cover. Young, complicated hair, make-up trowelled on, sneering, leathers. This was promising. I bought the magazine.

To this day, Joan Jett remains my ur-image of what a rock star should be. That do-not-give-one-simple-fuck look that defined her approach. A person who was above it all. I spent a lot of time staring at her picture. This was how I wanted to be.

At the time, I cared a lot about what other people thought of me. That was all I cared about.

I found most conversations excruciating because I felt I was going over poorly in all of them. Not smart enough or cool enough or simply with it enough. Not witty or informed. Other kids seemed to have the ability to bend people toward them. If they moved, someone would follow. I didn't have this. I had a few friends, but I moved alone.

Being alone is dangerous as a kid. If that reputation attaches itself to you, your next step is to become a victim.

There is something feral about the way children organize themselves. Everyone instinctively understands their status, but the pack is mutable. In some situations, with certain arrangements of people, you are accepted. Switch out a few of those and replace them with others, and people you thought were your friends no longer are. They've recognized someone of higher status and yours has diminished accordingly.

Lacking confidence and wearing that lack far too obviously, I wasn't able to figure out where I belonged. I drifted toward kids who didn't like me very much, and to groups in which I was only barely tolerated.

Joan Jett would not have put up with this sort of shit. You could tell that by looking at her. If you gave Joan Jett the gears, she would stab you.

I asked for a tape player for Christmas that year and for two cassettes—Joan Jett's and *Non-Stop Erotic Cabaret* by the British synth band Soft Cell. The title caused my mother to shoot me a look, but she left it.

Without understanding what I'd done, I had already arrived at the two polarities of musical fandom. There are the artists you want to be, and the ones you want to listen to. They often aren't the same.

I spent more time looking at Joan Jett than listening to her music. This was a sexless pursuit. Jett was far too imperious for me to objectify her. She was better than me. She was a life goal—"How to Stand Out."

Soft Cell was a different story—two gawky dweebs with bad hair wearing leather jackets that looked as if they'd been stitched together from garbage bags. I was not a cool person, so I could tell these two weren't either. However, they had recorded "Tainted Love," which may contain the most infectious pop hook in history. I didn't listen to the other nine songs on that album more than two or three times. I listened to "Tainted Love" until the cassette wore out.

The next stage of musical advancement was the *Smash Hits of the 70s* or *Biggest Rock Hits of the Year* collections. Racks of these could be found at the cut-rate department stores where my mother shopped.

This took guessing out of the equation. Someone had done the thinking for me.

There is no more golden moment in your formative years than the one that comes after you've discovered something but haven't yet had shame beaten into you. You don't know what you're *supposed* to like. No one has yet curled a lip when you announce, "Chilliwack is good" or "Journey is better than The Beatles."

I hadn't yet learned that as soon as things become ubiquitous, you are supposed to pretend to sneer at them. You've closed this circle whenever you come around to the right way of thinking of things—that there are no guilty pleasures. Only pleasures. That takes years and years, and you often end up right back where you started.

My next step up the ladder of musical maturation was Michael Jackson. Jackson was the forbidden fruit that helped me find shame. I loved him, but after a while learned to keep it to myself.

After that, Def Leppard. This was my first true concession to what others thought, rather than what I liked myself. Not that Def Leppard isn't a great band. But I came to them because it was clear to me that that was the done thing.

Unlike Jackson, Def Leppard was hard and more acceptable to my white trash peers.

Like all proper rock gods, they had a uniform you could copy. They wrote their name in a stylized font you could stencil onto your binder to advertise your affiliation. If you aren't in a gang, belonging to one or other musical tribe is the closest you get.

My mother was tolerant of my new mutability on the musical front, but that openness ended when I came home wearing the signature clothing item of Def Leppard's lead singer, Joe Elliott—a tank top emblazoned with the Union Jack.

There was a simple-to-follow line of political ethos that ruled my house—Britain bad; all other things up for argument. The Easter Rising. 1919. Provos. The Troubles. Pádraig Pearse, Michael Collins and all the rest. Those words meant something in my house. We were all volunteers in that fight whether we wanted to be or not, and should not be traipsing around cloaked in the dirty flag of the oppressor. No matter how great an album *Pyromania* was and remains.

If I could time travel back to ten moments in my life, that would be one of them. So I could give myself a slap for being such a taunting, ungrateful little schmuck.

My mother physically recoiled from that shirt. She was not an expressive person. She had the flat gaze that identifies the rural Irish more surely than any accent. Going back generations, those people had seen a lot. Today's disasters weren't going to surprise them.

So the way her face twisted up when she caught sight of that shirt froze me on the spot. She lifted a hand and pointed at me. Like she'd spotted a witch.

I'd seen this coming, but thought I might get away with it. I never did manage to get away with anything.

"What do you think you're doing?"

"I just . . ."

"No."

"I got it because . . ."

"Not in this house."

"But, I . . ."

"Take it off."

"But, it's . . ."

"Off."

I handed it over and stood there bare-chested and humiliated while she marched it out to the trash can.

After I'd saved up more money, I bought another. I'd leave the house in the morning in one t-shirt, put the Union Jack on in the bathroom at school and take it off when I got home again.

It wasn't exactly driving a safety pin through your nose, but it was the first puny punk rock act of my life. After a few weeks, it occurred to me that it wasn't terribly brave if I was too afraid to do it in front of my mother. So I stuffed the shirt down in a drawer and stopped wearing it. It disappeared soon thereafter.

Of course, she had known. How? No idea. But my mother knew everything. That was another basic principle.

I went to high school and all of this became far more important. Music was now tribal. What you liked determined where you belonged, and with whom. People now cared deeply about bands. These were real relationships.

For the first time, I found myself a proper girlfriend. A hang-out-at-each-other's-houses, talk-all-night-on-the-phone, occasionally-get-a-hand-under-the-shirt girlfriend. Her name was Sabrina. We were fourteen.

Sabrina liked me (sort of, I think), but she loved Metallica. If a member of Metallica had rolled up on us in her bedroom while I was fiddling with the clasp on her bra and told her to murder me on the spot, she'd have picked up a lamp and crushed my head like a melon.

She listened exclusively to Metallica. Even in uniform at a Catholic school, she was at all times wearing something that said *Metallica*—a sweatshirt, a patch on a jean jacket or a backpack. In civvies, she looked like she was in Metallica—everything black, skin-tight and severe. As a rule, she did not smile.

I can't remember what we used to talk about. She wasn't a warm or gregarious person (outside of discussing the hermeneutics of Metallica). I suppose it was the hair that fascinated me.

It is difficult to describe the ambition of Sabrina's hairdo. It was spiked off her head at impossible angles and to incredible lengths. But the real star was the bangs. She combed them down over her forehead, her eyes and her nose. The only visible part of her face was her mouth. She was Batman wearing a blond mask. Occasionally, in an effort to be romantic, I'd lean in and sweep her bangs away and look into her eyes. Which was when she'd hit me.

Sabrina made it clear that Metallica was a non-negotiable part of our relationship. They would have to become my favourite band, too.

So they did. I bought all the albums. I listened to them like homework. I found some biographical material and memorized the band's back stories. I got deep in a way I never had before.

Sabrina and I didn't last long. She dumped me for some heavy-metal aficionado in his twenties, the type we called a "handstand"—a skinny bastard with jeans painted onto his spindly legs and floppy white high-top sneakers. The sort of guy who looks like he's walking around on his hands.

I didn't miss her much, but she had had a profound influence on me. Metallica stuck. I started wearing a lot of black. I began to consider my hair and what it said about me.

The next year—grade ten—was my musical apotheosis. An actual one.

My cousin Paula was about ten years older than me—adult, but still young. I didn't see her often, but one day at her parents' house she told me to go downstairs and flip through her albums to see if anything caught my eye.

I was down in that basement for maybe a half-hour. I thought it presumptuous to put any of the records on. All I did was memorize titles. That half-hour defined the rest of my musical life.

The band that recurred most in Paula's milk-crate catalogue was one I had vaguely heard of but had never listened to—The Smiths.

The next weekend, I went downtown and bought a cassette tape of *The Queen Is Dead*. I went home, sat on my bed and slipped it into my Walkman.

The first song—the title song—kicks off with a shoddy recording of a vaudeville number. Drums come in urgently. A guitar holds a long discordant note. The song descends, rather than rises, into melody. And then Morrissey's posh, anguished whine floats the whole thing up symphonically.

I don't understand the trope of love at first sight, because it's impossibly shallow. But love at first listen? Absolutely. You recognize your music when you first hear it.

This was that, a perfect combination of style, tune, vocals, lyrics and, most importantly, manic-depressive outlook.

For years, I judged people on where they stood on The Smiths. Not knowing them was forgivable. Knowing, but not rating them was proof of a dire lack of cool and—only a kid could feel this strongly about something that does not matter—moral character.

If you were one of those people who thought The Smiths affected, simpering or mediocre, you were missing something basic—good taste.

I listened to that tape everywhere, but where I remember listening to it best was on the subway. On the route to school, the train would come briefly above ground in a few spots. I'd be standing into a doorway, turned away from everyone else, staring out the window.

The light would hit and I'd feel the core disconnect of my teen years—that whatever was happening in my world, right now (on the train—nothing) was so much less than whatever was happening out there in the big, brightly lit world (everything).

The Smiths were the soundtrack of that idea.

They are a band for people who suspect that life is going to disappoint them. Your girlfriend will fall into a coma, the flames will rise to your Roman nose, you'll be looking for a job and then you'll find a job, and heaven knows you'll be miserable then. If they incorporated and had to write a mission statement, it would be "What else did you expect?"

Morrissey armed me for all the letdowns to come, and assured me that I wasn't special in suffering them. He was the closest thing I've ever had to a life coach and he may be the greatest friend I've ever had.

I won't try to shame you into agreeing that The Smiths are the finest act in musical history (though they are). I cared about and was influenced by a disparate hodgepodge of their contemporaries (though some were not very like them at all)—The Cure, Joy Division, Suicidal Tendencies, Pink Floyd, U2, Tom Waits, Public Enemy, The Replacements, R.E.M., Hüsker Dü, the Eurythmics. . . . It's a long list.

But it was never again like hearing The Smiths for the first time. Because you're only fifteen once.

You will listen to other bands and like other songs, but nothing will ever connect you to a time and a place in the same way. Everything new will contain echoes of something old. School dances and all-ages clubs and the way you felt when you heard "Blue Monday" and came bouncing off the wall with all your friends at the same time. That can't be repeated. It's a small, necessary death.

SEX

LESS THAN I had hoped.

LOVE

THOUGH YOU WOULD LIKE to avoid the issue, eventually you will reach "women" on your grade school to-do list. What are they? How ought they to be approached? And who's going to fill you in on all of this?

Well, nobody. School will offer you a useless skill like geometry, but no one in a union job is going to teach a ten-year-old how best to flirt.

There was no help at home in this regard. My mother would rather have had a conversation about the family converting to cannibalism than one involving romantic notions. The few times I tried I got "the pose"—one leg slowly drawn over the other, the opposite arm folded over chest, hand holding tea mug in death grip, blank stare. And after a long while, if I could hold my courage, "I'm not sure what I can tell you about that." A vocal peak at the end to signal the conversation was over.

This was most likely a problem of semantics. I'm not sure how I posed these questions, but it was probably something along the lines of "Do girls like me?" or "Am I old enough to have a girlfriend?"

What could she say to that? Yes, son, you're a regular Douglas Fairbanks. I doubt anyone could resist you. I suppose there are mothers who say things like that—creepy, overly supportive things—but mine was a realist. I was going to have trouble with a few things in life—regular employment, social graces, public speaking—and you could add women to the list. In her defence, she never said it out loud—"You are a bit gormless." It was understood.

The introduction of romance as a going concern is the point at which all of us become midget anthropologists. We study the tribe. Record observations. Attempt to repeat what we have seen.

First, it's important to accurately assess your standing in the grade four hierarchy. One of the girls I went to school with was the daughter of a former Toronto Maple Leaf. In terms of stature, that was Everest to us. Everyone else was crowded together in a trailing pack. No one had any money. No one dressed well. None of us were particularly good looking. We each had to find our own niche.

Amongst the things that sociologists say determine a man's attractiveness to women is "success at games." (Perversely, it works the opposite way around for women.) I was not sporty, per se. Which is to say I was depressingly average at games. But this has its own social advantage because people who are good at games like playing games with people who are less good. This is the offshoot of sports called politics.

The only game we played in any organized fashion was a bowdlerized handball with rules more complicated than contract

bridge and a high incidence of physical brutality. We'd chalk out-
lines on a wall. The goal was to bounce the ball within them.
Simple enough.

But there were no "curvsies" (putting the ball at a near
right angle to the wall and into a neighbouring backyard) and
no "fakesies" (pretending to smash the ball and then tapping it
lightly, causing your opponent to run back to the wall with
such haste he ended up going into it face-first). Smashing was
called "smashing" and was allowed, but within limits that
changed depending on who you were playing and how they
were doing. One man's clean smash was another man's cheat.

A pack of us—ten, twelve boys—would start recess in a
huge, undulating handball mob and it would go off like
Thermopylae. People ramming into each other, clotheslining
opponents, rabbit punching guys as they passed. Often, the game
would end in a fist fight. It was so vicious we would have been
better off playing football with hockey sticks. By the time the
bell rang, it was something out of *Apocalypse Now*, with kids
dragging other semi-conscious kids back into class so they could
enjoy their concussions during geography.

I was a serviceable handball player (i.e., rugby tackler) and that
was noticed by important people. Important male people who
had good connections into the female sphere of the schoolyard—
the Michelles and Pattys and Jennifers who all terrified me. I was
moving up in the world.

The next stage was note passing.

Only a certain class of people could pass notes. No one told
you that. You just knew it.

Once you'd become that sort of person, you had to decide
what sort of note passer you would be. Were you a direct

sort—"I like you"? Were you a teaser—"I know someone who likes you"? Were you a coward—"Do you like me?"

Note passing was fraught with several layers of risk. Our teacher, Ms. Florio, was up there at the front like the Gestapo. She had nun-like detection instincts and several classroom snitches.

In order to get a note moved from one row to another, you had to catch someone's eye. And while you were highly invested in the operation's success and took great care, the next guy was somewhat less invested. Sure, he didn't want to be caught with the note, but he didn't give a damn if your urgent communication made it across the lines. This indifference was compounded each time the note was passed. In general, it was best to fall for a girl who was, at most, two desks over from you. If you were at the back and she at the front, you'd have been better off pining for someone in Poland.

Occasionally, Ms. Florio would intercept the note. She would not read it aloud. Instead, she'd identify the handwriting and then fix you with a look, giving everyone else permission to laugh at you.

Even when a note made it through, it could take an agonizingly long time. Kids dawdled, or read the note for themselves and smirked, or passed it to the wrong person, or put it in their desk for safekeeping. You'd have to follow each stage of this journey because it was vitally important that you be looking when the intended recipient unfolded and read your message. That's when you would know.

Girls sent a different sort of note around—an origami job meant to be played like "Eenie Meenie Minie Moe," ending up on one of several romantic outcomes. You were then to pass the note back with your (made-up) answer. The only point of this seemed to be to drive us boys mad with confusion, and it was notably successful in this regard.

During all of grade school I sent only one direct romantic missive, to a girl named Patty who I knew in my heart was too good for me, but hoped might be the sort to take pity.

The note read something along the lines of "I like you. Will you go to the dance with me?"

I saw her get the note. She glanced over at me, tilted her head and smiled sadly. Even in the moment I was thinking, "Remember that look. You'll be seeing it again in your life. Lots of times."

At recess, she handed me her own note—an alarming breach of classroom-only note-passing etiquette. It read—this part I remember precisely—"I like you as a friend."

Oh Lord, the humiliation. The wretched, wretched humiliation. I was ten years old and felt the weight of the Ancients upon me. While the other guys were maiming each other at handball, I hung on a fence, looking off into the distance like I'd just lost a brother in the war. Eventually, Patty came over to pat me on the shoulder while everyone stared, which was both cool and uncool of her.

I decided then never to try again.

Of course, I tried again. A whole bunch of different ways, most of them so subtle as to be indecipherable. Putting my faith in mind reading, I'd laugh a little too loudly around certain girls, or call them by their names too often, or try to hold a look too long.

Some people are smooth. I am not one of them.

I began to realize the point of entry was to get someone interested enough in you that they wanted to talk to you. You didn't want to do this in front of other kids. Someone was always watching and recording. Your best option was the home telephone.

You didn't need to ask for a number. Everybody I knew was in the phonebook. You also didn't need to ask permission to call. That request was implied when their mother picked up the phone and asked, "Who may I say is calling?"

If a girl didn't want to talk to you, they'd say that to their mother, who would in turn portentously tell you, "I'm afraid Lourdes can't come to the phone right now." You'd know you'd miscalculated and would never, ever call again. It was a less simple time, but probably better. There were multiple gatekeepers meant to protect feelings on all sides.

This all implies that I made these calls myself. In fact, I just *thought* about what it would be like to call a girl, what I would say and how it would go. Poorly, I supposed. Sometimes I'd dial six of seven numbers on a rotary phone, knowing full well I would not complete the task.

But I enjoyed the terrifying idea that my finger might slip mistakenly into the correct slot and accidentally pull it 180 degrees and find myself unable to take the receiver from my ear because static electricity had welded it in place. And then what?

The first woman who showed actual interest in me didn't roll onto the scene until I was in high school—Sabrina—who, on reflection, schooled me in many disciplines. "Interest" may be too strong a word.

She was awfully aloof and often ignored me entirely in the hallways, so our relationship was conducted on the phone in the evenings. There were hours and hours of that. Whole nights spent talking about nothing. Once, Sabrina went off and sat down to dinner with her family while I *waited* on the line. This was an early lesson in power imbalances and how not to handle them.

Sabrina had her own separate phone line—a wild extravagance. I had to pull the communal phone into my bedroom and lean against the door. Every ten minutes or so, my mother would come by and yell through it, "Are you still on the phone?!"

I'd say, "I'm almost done!" She'd stomp off and then we'd do it again. It was our thing.

My mother bought a second telephone for our line, and she'd pick it up at terrible moments—"Do you really like the way I do my hair? Really?"—and breathe into it for a while. The three of us—my mother, Sabrina and I—would sit there silently waiting for my mother to lose interest and hang up. I was always on guard for the "click" that meant someone was listening.

It was like East Berlin, but stupid.

I spent a lot of time as a teenager trying to imagine what certain things would *feel* like. I wanted to know how it would feel to live alone, or have money, or drive a car, or do heroin. I enjoyed spending long hours lying in bed casting myself forward in time to random ages and envisioning what life would look like. The highest I could ever get was thirty-five, at which point my life would either be settled or in disarray. I could see it going both ways. The idea of love, or passion, or fixation, did not come into it. It wasn't that I didn't think it possible. I couldn't think of it at all. Of course, there was a woman somewhere in this scenario, but she was obscure to me.

There wasn't much to model on in this regard. My mother never remarried. For a few years, my brother and I prepared ourselves for the possibility that one day we'd come home and there would be a strange man there fixing something in the basement or whatever it was normal fathers did, but when it didn't happen that vague anxiety faded.

My mother was my mother—a solitary unit, usually to be found lurking around a corner like a home invader, waiting to confront you about some chore you'd forgotten to do. She existed, as best I could tell, in just two states: out in the world working; or at home waiting.

This commitment to solitude did not seem, on its face, a wrong way to exist. All three of us could be in the house together, not interacting in any meaningful way, for hours at a time. It was often a serene place. And when it wasn't, matters could escalate to extreme "Get off the phone, now!" volumes.

So when I met Liz at the age of fifteen while we were both toiling at a downtown movie theatre, it was clear she was going to have to do the bulk of the work.

There is a trick of the brain that reduces all distant memories to either happy or wry ones, but I believe I did have remarkable good luck in first falling in love with someone like Liz. Though the same age as me, she was nominally my boss at the theatre. She was the thing that is most attractive in someone else—competent. She had her shit together in a way fifteen-year-olds are not supposed to. In Liz's world, all problems had solutions. In my world, all problems were the thin, precarious barrier separating you from even worse problems. If I was generally morose, Liz was cheerful. Relentlessly positive. Actually magnetic. The sort of person who seems an inch off the ground at all times.

She had the thing I had never before encountered in my interactions with the people closest to me—warmth. She was delighted to see you each and every time. She'd come rushing up to grab hold of you. When she talked, she reached out to brush her hand on your shoulder, or push you gently when she was amused. She was not afraid to embrace people—literally or figuratively—an idea which confounded me.

Liz was my gateway drug to intimacy in all forms. I would never be entirely like her. She was born with what she had. But I could be a little more like her. It didn't occur to me that Liz could *like* like me. That was still the word we used for such things—*like*. Not *love*, or *want*, or *is interested in*, which are all marketing terms. Someone *liked* you—a modest, reachable goal. Even once we had started dating—I'm not sure how that happened, it just did—I did not realize we were dating. We were just going places together and occupying the same proximate space for some duration.

There was nothing physical between us because, despite her touchiness in most situations, Liz was, like me, shy and inexperienced. Also, she was Greek, which is like a whole different species of human. More ancient and advanced.

Eventually, Liz's older sister, Betsy, who also worked at the theatre, had to take me aside for an excruciating talk.

"She'd like you to kiss her," the sister told me.

"Kiss her? Really? You're sure?"

"She told me."

"She told you *how*?"

"With words. Like a person. You should do that."

"Do what exactly?"

"Kiss her."

Betsy was dating a guy who was also Greek. He would often roll by the theatre at night to pick her up. He was built like a linebacker, had thick, ringleted hair that stretched down to his ass, drove a Camaro and was named—I am not even kidding here—Hercules.

Reasoning that someone who was dating Hercules must know a lot of things, I did as I was told. It was not my first kiss, but it was my first real one. It happened outside the theatre late one night, as Liz was about to leave, after a long and portentous lingering during which she knew what I was doing, and I knew that she knew what I was doing, and on like that, panoptically. I had felt this before, but never with another person. This was genuine intimacy. Time stretched interminably and I found myself considering the act as it was happening. You get only a few of these "falling off a building" experiences in life—where the act is so monumental that it starts a scroll reel in your mind of everything that led into it and a small, enlivening terror of what comes next. I suppose this is as close to pure Zen as any one of us gets. We are truly living in a moment.

My relationship with Liz was not mediated from a distance because I could not call her on the telephone. Her family was traditional Greek Orthodox and would not have appreciated a Catholic leching around their youngest daughter (this bush-league "forbidden love" trope made things that much more exciting).

Liz had about a dozen older brothers, and Betsy delighted in telling me how enthusiastically they would hospitalize me if they ever found me with Liz. I imagined Hercules fighting his way into and then back out of the living room every time he picked her up.

When I was feeling particularly emboldened, I'd tell Liz that I was just going to pop by one day and take my licks. I hoped she would see that I was brave. Like—and I just can't stop myself from writing this over and over again because it's that amazing—Hercules. I imagined her frantic, begging me not to take the chance.

But she would only say, "Don't do that."

"What's the worst they could do?"

"I once saw Spiros [or Mikonos or whatever this one especially vicious brother out of the bunch was called] break a guy's arm."

So I didn't do that.

Because we were forced to engage each other only in person, our relationship took on an oddly adult cast. We'd make dates to see each other for only a few minutes, outside subway stations halfway between our homes. I'd come to her after-school volleyball games and sit there with the other kids' parents.

We weren't playing at this. We had a life together. I was dependent on her attention and opinions, as I believe she was on mine. When I told her I was in love with her, she laughed and said, "Of course you are," and the way she said it was so much better than anything John Hughes had taught me to expect. Nothing dewy or affected. No need for Molly Ringwald tears. Liz's reaction was real.

My mother thought most of my friends dull-witted buffoons (like me, they were), but even she liked Liz. The first time they met, Liz hugged her, and my mother froze like an animal under attack. I'd never seen anyone hug my mother. I had certainly never seen my mother hug anyone else. Not a hugger in any way, shape or form. An active anti-hugger, my mother. But Liz blew right through her reticence. That was a part of Liz's magic—she assumed everyone wanted to be loved and touched and made to feel special. And all of us do.

One day, my mother put a framed picture of Liz up in the living room. Not a picture of Liz and me. Just Liz. (It did not occur to me until later that there was no picture of me up anywhere.) Unlike all my mother's other relationships, her connection to Liz was nothing but lightness. Occasionally, I'd come home and Liz would be there, unannounced, sitting in the kitchen with my mother. Standing in the foyer untying my shoes, I could hear my mother laughing. She never laughed. A part of me supposed I should be jealous—either of Liz loving my mother so much, or of my mother feeling the same way. But the feeling never took. As happy as I was for myself, I felt a different sort of satisfaction in bringing something so different and good into my mother's life. It may even have been the better of the two feelings, because it was generous.

This golden stage went on forever in terms understood by fifteen- and sixteen-year-olds—a year and a bit. Of course, it ended poorly and it was my fault.

I got a different job at a different theatre and Liz and I saw each other less. I began to realize that I was a person unsuited to intimate connections, no matter how much I depended on them. While craving closeness, I also chafed at it. I suppose (well, I know) that had something to do with the manner in which I'd grown up, and I could get all Freudian about it, but each person is like the universe. It is logically impossible to accurately consider a system of which you are a part. You cannot separate yourself from it in order to do the considering, because that would also be a function of the system. You are a closed loop of behaviours and, given time, you will always circle back to your base setting. Mine was "flee."

The ending was painful and, unlike every other part of our

relationship, dramatic. I came armed with a Hughes-ian script taken from *Sixteen Candles* about moving on and doing what was best, but Liz didn't want to hear it. She wasn't just angry with me, exactly, though she was that. Mostly she was confused by this person I had turned out to be. That was worse.

Since we had no good reason to run into each other—she lived on the other side of the city—we rarely saw each other again and never truly spoke. She married young and I trust is happy in her life. She was better than me in that way, and most others.

My mother took this all very hard. Which is to say that when I told her, she said, "How could you do something so stupid?" and never brought it up again.

She kept the picture of Liz up for months. When I once wondered about it—in the midst of an argument, of course—she barked at me that her pictures in her house were her business. But a few days later she took it down and I felt worse all over again.

I did not regret anything about being with Liz, being chosen by her. She hadn't taught me to love or anything so grand, but she'd given me the chance to prove to myself that I was capable of it. When you're young, that's something. You can build on that.

But the manner of the ending nagged at me. This was an entirely new feeling—truly disappointing people. Not by screwing up, which I had done plenty of before. But by volition. By setting out to do it knowingly.

Though you'd rather not, you take that with you, too.

HOOD ORNAMENTS

FOR CENTURIES, residents of the small Polynesian island of Yap traded with a currency they called rai. Rai are limestone discs. They look like calcified donuts. What makes the rai remarkable is its size. It varies, but tends toward enormousness. The biggest rai on record is twelve feet across and weighs four tons.

Obviously, you weren't going to drag your rai to the grocery store to buy cereal. The Yapese developed an oral tradition of possession. As long as everyone agreed that Jack's gigantic stone donut had become Jill's, it had. The stones were hard to come by and hard to carve with wooden tools, so the circulation remained low and value remained stable.

It sounds like a fair system and it worked for a long time.

Then a European sailor shipwrecked on Yap. He'd brought along iron tools, which made it much easier to carve new rai. That introduced a disastrous concept to the Yapese economy—inflation.

All this to say that just about anything—no matter how cumbersome or ridiculous—can be a unit of exchange. The value of money is a delusion. It only works as long as everyone agrees to share in it.

The guys I hung around with didn't have much money. We all had part-time jobs, but we spent those earnings on essentials— hamburgers, drugs, cigarettes, subway tickets and liquor. Amongst my group of friends this created a pleasingly flat society. We didn't prize certain brands. There was no new phone to obsess over. The only statement piece of electronics any of us had was a Sony Walkman, and everyone had the same basic model. No one person had more than any other. It was a stable micro-culture. So, like the sailor and the Yapese, we had to ruin that.

One night at a bush party, someone showed someone else something they'd stolen on the way over—a hood ornament. It was the Chrysler emblem—a cheap, plastic, five-pointed star. He'd probably taken it off a K-car, which was ubiquitous at the time. It was the Honda Civic of its day, except gruesomely ugly and famously unreliable.

In the mid-eighties, just about every vehicle had a hood ornament. We decided that we wanted them all.

A good question here is, "Why hood ornaments?" And the only answer is, "It's hard to say. We weren't very bright." I presume it had something to do with Public Enemy and Flavor Flav's penchant for clock necklaces. Insignia were a big deal. That's probably what we thought of these things as— medallions that could never be worn.

And just like that, hood ornaments became the unit of exchange between a group of eight or ten of us.

Plainly, this was both theft and vandalism. That didn't bother us. These people had things we wanted—cars—and we did not. Why was that fair? This wasn't crime. It was socialism in action. We were balancing the scales.

We spent whole nights at this, prowling the side streets in and around High Park looking for new logos to expand our collections. We traded them amongst ourselves. We kept our own oral tradition of who had what, and who was winning.

Some of these were easy to get off—the K-car's in particular. That was attached to the hood by a thin wire. You could yank it off with a strong flick of the wrist. One of my friends was so good at it, he could take the ornament off a car idling at a red light as he crossed, then run off before the driver realized what had happened.

Others were emblems attached to the hood with metal hooks. You needed a knife or a pry bar to get at those.

Some were welded on. Those required a metal file and a long time. After a while, we were going out on Friday nights weighed down with more tools than a carpenter.

As your collection expanded, your status within the group increased. Once everyone had reached a critical mass, you needed prize pieces to stand out. My signature item was the metal ram off a Dodge pickup. It had taken me the better part of an hour, sawing at it in a driveway in the middle of the night.

There was a rumour amongst us that someone on the Kingsway owned a Rolls-Royce that they parked on the street at night. Getting that winged angel would have represented the peak. We never could find that car, if it actually existed.

Stealing the ornaments was a completely pointless thing to do, which even then I think we realized. But no one wanted to be left out of the gang, so everyone participated. We thought it harmless enough.

One night, we were at it on one of the small streets that we took each day to get to school. There were three of us. It was winter. We'd been drinking. It was no longer fun. It was just something we did, mindlessly. We'd taken dozens that night.

We made our way up to the bus terminal at Runnymede subway station. It was late-ish. Ten o'clock maybe. I always had my eye on my watch, since my mother's midnight curfew was ruthlessly enforced. If I showed up late, the deadbolt was thrown and I'd have to spend the night on the porch.

Working on the theory that nothing good happens after 12 a.m., it was an effective deterrent to letting a bad night drift into a disastrous one. But I still had a couple of hours. We were heading off to meet someone else.

I heard the police cars coming into the station at speed, sirens going, tires skidding.

I remember thinking, "What poor bastard are they after?"

I didn't turn to look, so the hand on my shoulder took me by surprise.

Since I hadn't seen him yet, it didn't register that this was the law. The cop spun me around. As he did so, I swung instinctively. As with most punches, it didn't come anywhere close to the target. The blow glanced off his shoulder.

But he was not happy with me. Once I saw the uniform, I went slack. He was bigger than me, adult, much stronger. I could tell that from his grip. He dragged me over to the hood of his car and threw me across it. That didn't hurt. Then he picked me up by the collar of my jacket, marched me back a couple of steps and tossed me into the door. That one hurt.

When you are fighting, everything blurs into a haze of fear and rage. Mostly fear. You're not thinking anything. That's the

difference between people who can fight and people who can't—
the ability to overcome panic.

But when you are in the midst of a beating, your mind slows
and things get clear. You surrender.

Years later, when I read Chuck Palahniuk's *Fight Club*—a
celebration of a particularly masculine type of ritual suffering—it registered deeply with me. There is something freeing
about absorbing punishment.

You don't take a beating. You endure it. That can be strangely
satisfying.

The cop didn't go so far as to punch me, but he was intent
on running me into a bunch of things until he got tired. They
wedged the three of us in the back of their squad car and left
us alone. Without saying anything to each other, we began
emptying our pockets. We shoved dozens of hood ornaments
and several tools down the back of the seat.

None of us had ever been in a police car, and so didn't realize
the rear seat cushion is removable. A different cop took us out
of the car, pulled out the cushion, nodded at the pile of metal
and said, "Whose is this?"

We all shrugged.

Coursing with adrenaline, I wasn't scared.

Two more cars arrived. We were split up. As one of my
friends was being hustled into a different back seat, he shouted,
"Don't tell them anything."

Like we were gangsters or something. This was turning into
criminal fantasy camp.

My cops drove me around for a bit. They pretended to be
angry. At one point, the car stopped suddenly and the cop in the
passenger seat got out, flung open the back door and poked at

me with his nightstick while I cowered against the door. We were both play-acting. I nearly laughed.

They asked where I'd done it. Was it this car? Or this car? Were you here? Was it your friend who did it? Which one? Just tell us, and you can go home. One of your friends already told us it was you.

Then I did laugh. Did this ever work?

First, I'd taken the beating like a man. Now I was going to be able to truthfully tell people at school that we'd been asked to rat each other out, and had refused. These cops were gifting us a massive reputational boost.

Finally, they brought us all to the station. It was late now. I'd missed curfew.

They processed us, took fingerprints. We were put in holding cells. They brought us out and took down our information. Our names were written on a greaseboard. Beside mine it said, "Assaulting an officer." Even that didn't bother me.

Then a cop said to me, "Your mother will be here soon."

"You didn't have to call her."

"Yes. We did."

Now I felt fear.

They brought me out through a loading bay. My mother was waiting there. The sight of her emboldened me.

"These guys hit me," I said, sounding a lot less tough than I'd have liked.

My mother—a tiny woman—looked up at the cop and said, "Is that true? Did you hit him?"

The cop still had me by the arm.

"He struck a police officer," he said.

"I don't care," my mother said. "Did you hit *him*?"

The cop smirked at me and let go of my arm. I don't blame him in the least. I was an insufferable little prick hiding behind my mother's skirts.

My mother chested up to the cop. Her chin was just above his belt.

"Did you hit him?"

"Well, I didn't," the cop said.

"What's your name?"

We were all in the parking lot by now. The cop backed away from us until he was inside the bay and hit the button that drew down the garage door.

As we stood there in the cold alone, it occurred to me that my mother had walked here. She'd have got up to a ringing phone and then left my eleven-year-old brother alone in his bed. There were no buses at this time of night. She had no car. It was well below freezing. It would've taken her an hour or more to get there.

"That was great," I said, meaning it.

She threw me a look I have never forgotten. It was something beyond disappointment. It was resignation. Like she was seeing me for the first time and realizing she didn't like me very much.

"If you ever do this again, don't call me," she said. "You can figure your own way out of it."

She didn't ask me if I'd done it. She knew I had. We walked home without speaking.

There were charges—public mischief. I suppose the assault bit was never filed.

As a young offender, I was granted a lawyer. I spoke to him once at his office. He was in a hurry and didn't explain anything to me. I never did ask. I didn't care to know.

I went back to school on Monday and made a meal of the story, playing down the key beats in the hopes people would think me modest and more dangerous.

A few months later, we all had to go to court. I'd been told to expect probation and community service. It didn't register. I had detached myself from the process. Whatever was going to happen was going to happen. Why worry? What did it matter in the grand scheme?

After the arrest, the three of us stopped collecting hood ornaments. I went home and threw out the ones I had (I guess I thought the house might be raided). With a third of its financial community having gone bust, our small hood ornament economy collapsed. Nobody cared about them anymore. In short order, no one could remember why we had in the first place. It had been tulip mania, but much stupider.

The lawyer came out to explain what would happen in court—a short trial and a quick judgment. He left.

He came out again and took my mother and me to the side. Things had changed. The charges were being dropped.

What luck. I was relieved, smiling.

The lawyer looked over at me and curled his lip. I realized that he did not like me.

He explained that the reason the case had been dropped was because there had been only one witness, a man who'd seen us stealing hood ornaments that night and called the police. In the intervening months, he'd seen us again. And again. We were hard to miss—big, loud, a lot of black leather, always moving in a pack. We walked by his house often. We hung out at a Harvey's just up the road. We didn't know who he was, but he knew us.

If he came to court, that would change. He'd thought better of the whole thing. In the end, he cited fear as his reason for backing out. My lawyer made sure I knew that.

There was a brief proceeding in court as the matter was ended. It was all very routine. Everyone looked busy and bored.

As we left, I caught up to my lawyer as he rushed off, and said, "Can you tell that man that we're sorry."

He stopped, turned and for the first time gave me the full weight of his attention.

"You're not to go near him," he said. "That would be very serious. That would be jail. Do you understand that?"

I said I did and he left.

My friends were skulking away with their mothers. We left without speaking to each other.

I never did find out who that man was. I'd see people on the street and think, "Him? Him?"

We would have nothing in common, he and I. But I knew what it was like to be scared. The worst part is the anticipation. Thinking that it's not going to happen today, but knowing it will happen at some point. Fear is corrosive. It's far worse than whatever you're afraid of.

I stopped walking down the usual streets and went the long way around. Reconstructing the night in my mind and what happened when, I could make a rough guess which of twenty or thirty houses was his. I didn't want him to see me and think that I was stalking him.

I started to dress differently, wearing colour again. Part of this was the occasional shedding of skin that is such a large part of growing up, but I also wanted to appear different in case he saw me. At best, he'd no longer recognize me. At least, I might seem less threatening.

I would like to have met him and apologized. Not for the cars or the crime. If I'm being honest with myself, that didn't seep through. I'd done it, just barely got away with it and learned my lesson. Not that it was wrong to do, but that it was monumentally foolish. I never did anything like that again.

What I wanted was a cleansing. First, to free him from worry. And then, to receive his absolution.

I never did get what I wanted. Just as well. I didn't deserve it.

WORK

WE ALL LIVE IN THE GREY, but at some point you have made a decision about whether to point in the general direction of darkness or light.

My incipient criminality wasn't hindered by any moral code. It just happened that I was very bad at it. I was the muppet who always got caught.

When we were teenagers, the cops would often stop us on the street for a speculative chat. We had that look.

One night, aged about fifteen, I had a very large bottle of vodka in my backpack. I was headed somewhere—doubtless, a park—with my friend Ned.

Had I played it cool, it would've been fine. I could not play it cool. When one of the cops asked what I had in the bag, I instinctively jerked it off the ground where I'd laid it protectively between my legs and threw it over my shoulder.

"Nothing," I squealed.

Of course—of course—I'd forgotten to close the top of the pack. As I swung the bag round, the bottle launched from it like a cruise missile. It was thrown with sufficient force that it took a good two or three seconds to arc through the air and then shatter on the sidewalk twenty feet away. It made a very unsatisfying "pop."

The cop looked at me. I looked at the cop. The cop looked at his partner. His partner looked at him. Ned looked at me. I could not look at Ned.

Then the cops started laughing, bent-over, hands-on-knees, gasping-for-air laughing.

It went on like that for a while. People walked by and joined in. Ned and I shifted from foot to foot. The cop finally recovered and put a hand on my shoulder to nudge himself back up to vertical.

"Go home," he said.

They left. We did not go home. We went to get more vodka.

One of the joys of being a teenager is that you have no sense of proportion. Everything you do, you do too much.

My moment of greatest temptation arrived when I was seventeen years old.

I had always worked. It was an expectation in my house that you had a job. I delivered the newspaper in grade school. In high school, I thought I could take a little breather. The day I announced that I'd made the football team was the day my mother rejoindered that that was going to get in the way of my as-yet-undiscovered after-school job. I quit football and got a gig on the fry line at a burger joint.

In the course of a year, I lit my hair on fire, cut myself constantly and suffered numerous contact burns. No amount of showering could rid me of the smell of being singed. My minimum-wage salary was largely spent on cigarettes, alcohol and painkillers.

The next summer I got a job at the Canadian Baseball Hall of Fame, housed at a sprawling lakefront amusement park called Ontario Place. This job was less dangerous. They had a batting cage (where you ducked swinging bats) and a pitching installation (where people insisted on throwing while you collected the balls).

It cost a couple of bucks to throw five balls and test your velocity against a radar gun. Most of the suckers who had a go were young guys trying to impress girlfriends or middle-aged guys trying to impress their kids. This often ended poorly.

I'd try to help.

"It's probably a good idea to warm up a bit first."

Nobody wanted to warm up. Everybody wanted their initial effort to hit the red line.

We are used to hearing what major league pitchers throw—mid-eighties at the low end. Those numbers are burned into the average man's brain. A regular person cannot throw a ball eighty miles per hour. Not even close. But Christ did they try.

A peculiarity of the pitching motion is that it works best when done loosely. The secret is mechanics rather than strength. Generally speaking, the harder you try, the poorer the results.

Guys would get up there, give their kid a wink, wind up like Nolan fucking Ryan—knee up in the air, the whole bit—fire one in, look over at the gun and see the number "57."

It was at this point they'd say, "I think the gun is broken."

"No, sir. The gun is not broken."

"I know I throw faster than that."

What I should have said was, "And how, pray tell, would you know that? From your time in the New York Mets organization?"

But I'd just shrug.

They'd cycle from embarrassment to anger. That's when they'd get hurt—the throw right after a 57.

In a couple of months, I witnessed more muscle tears than a kinesiologist sees in a career. You could tell straight off. The body spasm. The off hand shooting up to the shoulder. The small dip in the knees and arch of the back. The panicked look over to the girlfriend/wife/son/daughter—did they see that?

Of course they did.

Were they ashamed?

Of course they were.

To a man, every one tried to play it cool: "Should've warmed up a bit more."

Some even finished their bucket.

In one instance, there was an audible "snap" and a whole drama with paramedics and down-on-the-ground writhing.

There was a chalkboard alongside the register where we kept track of the fastest throws of the day and the season. The best I ever saw was a young guy who was clearly an actual ballplayer. He bought ten buckets of balls. He lobbed the first nine of them in like he was shooting free throws. On the tenth, his arm stroke didn't look much different. But the gun was now up in the mid-eighties.

As I put his number up in the marker, he gave me a little nod and left. He'd come in alone.

On many days, the top aspirant was a woman. Because, like the actual pitcher, they weren't trying so goddamned hard to impress anyone. They just did it. This was the Nike motto evidenced in life. I made a mental note.

I couldn't help but notice something else as well. When you're handing over small change in return for a bucket of balls, no one expects a receipt. You can punch in "No sale," the register opens, you take the money, but no transaction is recorded. Eventually, it dawned on me that this was a business opportunity. For every five dollars I took in, one began making its way into my pocket. Who'd know?

Well, everyone.

I hadn't the sense to keep a mental tally of my illicit gains and make one withdrawal late in the day to decrease my exposure. Every time I made five dollars, I took the dollar.

At first, I was careful in how I managed the theft. Gradually, I got less careful. By the end, I was cheerily opening the register with a crowd around and helping myself.

The crucial thing I lost sight of was that the open-concept facility had two levels. I worked on the main. My boss worked on the second. The door to his office exited onto a walkway that directly overlooked the pitching station.

After too many weeks to credit, I was called up for a meeting. The boss asked if I was stealing. I admitted it straight off.

He hadn't been prepared for that. There was a long moment of silence.

"Then I guess I have to fire you," he said. "I really wish I didn't have to do this," he said.

"No, no, it's okay. I understand."

"I hope you're not angry with me," he said.

"No, not angry at all. I'd fire me too. Seriously. It's fine. I'm fine." (It was becoming clear that he wasn't going to get the law on me, and I relaxed.)

Then he started to cry.

He was a gentle guy I'd always liked.

When you are young, everyone around you seems old; when

you get older, everyone seems young. His name was Boyd. I imagine him now having been in his fifties, but he was probably much younger. I was a goofy kid with silly hair, but he'd treated me like a fully functioning human adult. I appreciated that. And now this.

He cried without embarrassment.

In my world, people smouldered when they got upset. They didn't weep or apologize. They didn't submit. The whole production deeply unsettled me. I left him leaning against his desk and walked out without saying anything to my co-workers, all of whom seemed to know what was going on.

I wasn't too bothered about losing the job. It was a shit job. There were always plenty of shit jobs around. But I was bothered that I'd let someone down.

I went home, told my mother I'd quit—"Why?" "It just wasn't for me"—and got another job at a local movie theatre.

It was the Runnymede on Bloor—the same place I'd had my *Star Wars* epiphany. It was an old, regal place. Red velvet furnishings, a balcony, double winding staircases. It had class.

The professional life of the theatre (so-called) suited me. It may have been the first thing I was ever good at, and certainly the first thing anyone else recognized me as being good at.

I switched the Runnymede for an art house downtown called the Cumberland. This is when work became my obsession—perhaps the only one that has ever repaid the effort.

I went to school and I slept at home, but I lived at the Cumberland. I took tickets, worked the cash, swept the halls, cleaned the toilets, schlepped popcorn and settled disputes. Eventually, they made me an assistant manager. They told me to go out and buy a suit. I hadn't the cash on hand to do so and was in the midst of one of my occasional silent periods with my mother.

We had a nice routine down—three full days from initial fight to eventual conversation. In the interim, we ignored each other entirely. I had to bend early in order to borrow the suit money. I can still recall my mother's look as I made my approach. She had the decency not to smile, but her eyes widened in triumph. We never again spoke of it, but it was understood that I had lost. In perpetuity.

There were many wonderful moments of growth and discovery at the Cumberland, but what I enjoyed most were the fist fights. There is something about a crowded movie theatre that pushes reasonable citizens toward insanity. A theatre is essentially a series of lines—the line for tickets; the line for snacks; the line to get into the auditorium. Often, by the third line, people are ready to snap.

There were fights in the alley; fights on the escalator; but most often there were fights at the door to the theatre. That's when people had reached their limit and wanted very badly to hit someone.

One guy dumped a box of popcorn over my head outside a matinee showing of *Music Box*. He was trying to very unsubtly jump the line and took offence when I blocked his way. He lacked the courage to hit me. Hence, the popcorn. In the movies, people are constantly hitting each other right in the nose. This is a pernicious fiction.

The head moves quickly. Your fist has a long way to travel, so, often, you end up hitting an ear, or the empty space where the head was when you started drawing your arm back.

But Popcorn Man could not believe that I would actually hit

him. Even as my arm was coming forward, he continued in this delusion. He remained stock still as I nailed him right below the eye, knocking him flat on his back. It remains the best punch I've ever thrown.

He said he would he call the police. But I was the guy in the suit now. I offered to walk him to the phone. I gave him my mother's smile. He gave up and left.

Another time, some complaining schmuck looked over my shoulder and bellowed, "I want to talk to the manager."

What may have been the sweetest three seconds of my then short life passed before I said, "Sir, I am the manager."

I think "drunk with power" covers it.

Childhood can be an extended exercise in powerlessness. You don't do things. Things happen to you, often without any explanation. At best, this creates resilience. You learn to adapt to changing situations. At worst, it enfeebles you. You grow used to allowing life to run you over.

The Cumberland mattered because it was the first place in my life where I was in charge of what went on. If the money was short, that was my problem. If someone had a complaint— and there were a lot of complaints—that was also my problem.

At first, I tried to solve people's problems. But it dawned on me that that wasn't really what they wanted. What they wanted was a chance to moan, to a captive audience. What they wanted was someone to listen to them.

I'd always been more of a listener than a talker. I could spend an hour listening to someone complain about the poor sound quality in Cinema 3. Direct eye contact, a slight tilt of the head, an occasional nod. In exceptional cases, I'd reach out and lightly brush a shoulder reassuringly. We'd agree that this—whatever "this" was—was a travesty that could never happen again. If it was going to happen again (like, I couldn't rewire the sound system for kicks on a Sunday), we'd agree that the corporation was rapacious and evil and we were both its victims. Then I'd give them free passes and we would part friends. I found these interactions immensely satisfying. While other things in my life were going wrong, they sustained me.

The spoils of the work were not quite as fulfilling. I made six bucks an hour, which is just as bad as it sounds now. I blew most of it on . . . well, I have no idea.

An enormous amount of cash passed through my hands. On a given night, it was many thousands of dollars.

Since I had no real life outside the theatre, I was often the last man in the building. Just the money and me.

The head manager was a decent sort and exceptionally lazy. Many of the things he should have been doing himself he delegated to me.

I followed him to a larger theatre, the Uptown. This was the jewel of Toronto theatres, a capacious venue that was more of an auditorium than a movie house. It was so vast there were feral cats living backstage.

One day, the manager instructed me to rid the place of them. They'd grown bold and were now hassling people during showings. I thought they added character to the place. I was overruled. I followed one into its lair—a large wooden tube laid behind the screen to aid in sound distribution. Once I got in there on my hands and knees in the pitch black, the cats attacked en masse and set me to shrieking flight. I told the manager that if he wanted to get rid of the cats, he ought to think of buying a flamethrower.

I continued to work small scams. At the time, tickets for the Toronto Film Festival were sold off a roll, like carnival ducats. While I worked the door, it was a simple business to pocket a few at one venue, walk a few blocks to another, sidle up to people in the ticket buyers' line and offer them the chance to jump the queue. I learned not to be greedy about it and I didn't think of it as theft. I preferred to see it as a yearly bonus. Plus, this was a service. These people wanted to see an incomprehensible Czech movie about manically depressed dockworkers and I could make that happen for them. What a mitzvah.

But the biggest event I worked at the Uptown was the opening of the original Batman film. The hype was astronomical. The crowds were frothing. It was a mad weekend, shows from early morning to late at night, all of them rammed with people.

There were two safes on the premises— a "petty cash" safe in the manager's office and a main safe in the atrium of the theatre. The main safe was in a public space for the sake of security—no robber could break in and trap you with it. This had happened before, with awful results.

Cash was counted in the manager's office and a small amount of it was held aside for the sake of change and cash-register floats. The bulk of it was taken upstairs to the atrium for deposit.

The main safe had two mechanisms—an outer door that was opened via combination lock and an inner door that required two keys, one held by the head manager and the other by Brinks. There was a slot in the inner door through which you could push envelopes of cash.

Usually, we carried the envelopes up in a plastic shopping bag. But usually, the theater calmed at night. On this heaving weekend, there were people in the building from daybreak until after midnight. No one wanted to take the chance of bringing the cash up and losing an envelope in the crush. So the money piled up in the petty cash safe downstairs.

Very late on Sunday night, there were only two of us left— the manager and me. He should've done the business himself but, as usual, he wanted to get home. He asked me to tidy and take up the money from the petty cash. Then he left. The night cleaners hadn't yet arrived. I was alone in the building. When I opened the petty cash safe, it was like a Scrooge McDuck fever dream. It was the size of a shallow bookcase. And it was full of money. Absolutely full.

I put it all in shopping bags. There was so much, I couldn't get it all up in one trip. I also couldn't leave any money lying around in either spot and didn't care to take most of it back out of the bags and replace it in the safe. So I dragged it all up the winding stair in short stages. When it was finally piled in front of the main safe, I sat down cross-legged on the filthy carpet in front of it. Close to $250,000. I'd need to work twenty full years to make this much money.

It was Sunday night. Brinks didn't arrive until Tuesday morning. Until Brinks came, no one could know the contents of the safe. It was Schrödinger's safe until then.

It's possible that Brinks wouldn't even notice the discrepancy until they'd reported back their counts (the money was expected to match up with slips deposited through the same slot—slips I was now holding). I wasn't scheduled to work again until Thursday, so no one would miss me. I'd have a thirty-hour head start at least.

I was seventeen years old. I didn't have a driver's licence. I couldn't remember where my passport was. I had no idea where I would go, or why, or what I would do there. Even in the moment, it occurred to me that a teenager walking around with a duffel bag full of loose cash in small denominations might be a little suspicious. I'd almost certainly be caught.

But I sat there and thought about it for a long time.

Then I put the money in the safe and went home.

I told my mother that story in abundant detail, concentrating on the part at the end about my deliberations. I suppose I wanted to be congratulated on having done the right thing. What was the point of doing good if no one saw you doing so? And what could be more salutary than a teenage idiot giving up hundreds of thousands of dollars for the sake of The Law?

"You were right," my mother said. "You shouldn't steal. Not for less than a million dollars. There's no point if it's less than a million dollars."

"It wasn't a million dollars."

"That's what I'm saying," she said, annoyed now. "You were right."

"So it would have been okay if it was a million dollars?"

"Well, I suppose that's for you to say."

"And then you'd never see me again or I'd go to jail?"

"I'm sure you would have been fine," my mother said.

It was becoming clear to me that while she didn't think I should have taken the money, she was just a little disappointed that I'd lacked the steel to do so.

I went on to work a lot of bad jobs—selling encyclopedias door to door, landscaping, phone sales, data entry, on the line at an auto parts plant. For the last few years, I've had some very good jobs.

Beyond the money, one never struck me as any more important or rewarding than any other. I've never quite understood the concept of "finding out what you are good at." You can be good at anything. So do that. The problem is that we have been sold the idea that only a few jobs are worth being good at. It's a regrettable scourge of our gilded age and probably results in more low-grade misery than any other thing.

My mother taught me that the only value of work is that it's work. You do it because you have to and because, if you do it right, it gives you some small sense of purpose. That's the reward. If you need more, you will be either enormously successful or, far more likely, enormously disappointed.

I consider myself lucky. I reached that understanding early.

NOTRE DAME

IN THE NORMAL RUN OF A LIFE, a sports team is something you inherit. Your father rooted for a particular side and so do you. Or your older brother did. In this sense, it's like a career in law or Communism—you do it without thinking too hard because everyone else is doing it. Maybe you don't agree with every little thing about this team. Maybe they've screwed up the draft for ten straight years. Maybe you're not on board for most of it. But there are cool uniforms and you had to pick, so there it is.

Contrary people pick a team for the opposite reason—because it's the one everybody they care about hates. That's the purest sort of sports love, one expressed in abeyance of good sense and in the full knowledge that it will make you a pariah in your own home. That's commitment, but once you've gone down that path, it's hard to come back. You're going to turn into "that guy," the guy who will argue that while climate change is almost certainly happening, scientists have been wrong before and it's important to keep an open mind.

Once you've made your decision, fandom becomes an infection. Like syphilis. You catch it from over-proximity to others, it takes control of your nervous system and eventually it drives you insane.

I was not cut out to join things. Joining means you are on a team. You're of one mind. Which I have some issues with straight off. You're looking around the room thinking, "Okay, that one over there. He looks all right. I'm fine with him. But that one? No. That's not going to work. I'm not with him."

There's a risk that you will realize too late that the whole thing doesn't suit you. You didn't want to be part of this in the first place (very like the final stages of Communism). But it's too late now. You bought the jersey.

Once or twice a year, my mother would take us to Maple Leaf Gardens with tickets she'd been given at work. Live NHL hockey in Toronto was a less bougie, more interactive experience in the seventies. The Leafs were unwatchable and so people had to find other ways to entertain themselves for three hours.

By the third period, they were drunk, surly and bored, and would begin beating the hell out of each other. During one of our rare excursions, a fight got so bad in the stands that play was halted. Out on the ice, the players from both teams leaned their chins on their sticks and watched the brawl as the cops waded in.

It was exciting and terrifying and I didn't really want anything to do with it. I wasn't that invested.

I have only loved one team, a brief, intense and ultimately bitter love—the University of Notre Dame football team.

I had no connection to that college, that place or its teams. Nobody in my family knew or cared about them. Nobody I knew played football or watched it. I didn't understand even the most basic elements of the game until I joined my high-school team when I was sixteen. I'd just switched over to this school because it was closer to home and my best friend, Brian, went there. It was a "technical" high school, which meant it had an emphasis on trades. It had a much stronger emphasis on minding your own fucking business.

One of my classmates was a convicted murderer. A guy on the football team was shot dead in a drug deal gone wrong. There was a notorious stickup gang that had deep roots into the student body.

I don't want to oversell this point. It was a rough school, but that roughness had an order to it. You didn't go there every morning in fear. Unlike most other schools, which were filled with people pretending to be dangerous, these kids actually were, and so felt relieved of the burden to be constantly proving it. In its way, it was an idyllic ecosystem for a teenage boy. As long as you didn't overstep or go out of your way to insult someone, you'd probably be all right.

You could further insulate yourself from random violence by being part of a group. Obviously, you weren't going to walk up to a bunch of guys on Day Three and say, "I'm with you now. Brothers 'til the end of time!"

That's what a football team is for. It's a gang that has to take you.

As a player, I was okay. Right in the middle somewhere. Though not fast or athletic, I was big. Football at the high-school level is forgiving of that type, at least in Canada.

It's a cerebral pastime, in the sense that you have to think about what you're doing before you do it. I played on the offensive line, where there is little place for instinct. You are given plays and have to remember exactly where to go and in what order.

I had no feel for this and was often lost during games. I'd limit myself to keeping track of the hut number, then rush out and hit the first person I saw. That usually worked.

Occasionally, it didn't. I was knocked unconscious twice, and both times by my own teammates. I'd gone the wrong way and caught a charging helmet in the side of the head. You'd get dragged off the field and sit out a series. The coach would come over after a while and grab you by the waist—an oddly romantic gesture—and say, "You okay?"

There was only one right answer. It was a different time, and I'm not willing to say it was any worse. We were encouraged to feel like soldiers out there.

What I loved about football was the tribalism. I'd been on hockey and baseball teams. Those were loose agglomerations of people who felt no real attachment to each other. They were hierarchical—the good players stuck together and the scrubs got ignored. You didn't feel protected by those people. You knew your place and, as a result, didn't invest yourself.

Football wasn't like that. The fear of getting hurt and the unspoken desire to hurt someone else stitched us together in a society without leaders. We were a big, ugly mob. It was as close as I ever hope to get to war, and that is intoxicating. I'd never felt so much a part of something.

The coach called us a family, and somehow that penetrated my cynicism. I didn't know these guys, but out on the field I loved each one of them. I gave in to it as I have rarely given in to anything. It was surrender.

We played on Fridays, but that wasn't enough for me. I wanted more football in my life.

I had to pick a team to support. The NFL seemed too obvious. So I went the college route. I don't know why I settled on Notre Dame. It was probably as simple as the nickname—the Fighting Irish. This was in the late eighties. Notre Dame was a Catholic cult in the United States, a bulwark against the forces of discord and evil (i.e., the University of Miami).

Sports fandom is like signing up for the military. You know from the outset that it will take you decades to advance through the ranks. You aren't the conqueror or even a colonist. You're an immigrant.

I didn't fall for Notre Dame. I jumped in. I'd made my decision and now this had to happen quickly.

So I found a couple of t-shirts and a Joe Montana practice jersey. I bought a jacket with the team's logo, a sparring leprechaun, emblazoned garishly across the back.

And I studied. I taught myself the mythology—Knute Rockne, the Four Horsemen, Touchdown Jesus. I subscribed to the team's monthly newsletter, *Blue & Gold*.

This all happened within the space of a few weeks. One day, I was a casual fan of several teams. The next, I was a panting obsessive for just one.

My brother, Brendan, would've been about twelve at the time. He was a golden child—good at school, great at sports, a bright light. He was at ease in the world. To Brendan, everything was going to work itself out.

I was morose and cynical. I didn't care about things, at least not in a way anyone could see. I got up, went to school, went to work, came home and did it again. My mother and I were most likely to argue when I was in the house, so I avoided being there. I was already grinding my way through life.

Maybe that's what drew Brendan to Notre Dame as well. It may have been the first thing he ever saw me invest myself in, and so wanted to encourage that. He had that way.

So, Day Zero—no Notre Dame

Day 30—Notre Dame

Day 45—Brendan notices me reading *Blue & Gold* in the living room and says, "What's that?"

Day 60—We are both bigger Notre Dame fans than someone whose alumni attachment to the university predates Reconstruction.

It was true that we had talked to each other before this. I suppose we must have, since we slept in the same room for many years. We certainly fought, often viciously.

When he was very little, I had terrible nightmares. Most often, they involved being locked in a basement with a barred window that looked out onto a long, dirt road. After a bit of fretting, I'd hear footsteps coming toward me through the dark. It was a garden-variety Freud/Jung/*Jaws* mashup.

Every night, I'd make my way into my mother's bed. One night, she tired of this routine. She yelled at me to get out. So I went back into my room, picked Brendan out of his bed and carried him into mine. I made him my only stuffed toy.

It didn't last long, since he didn't enjoy being smothered for half the night by someone twice his size. Though he'd done me a favour, I resented him for that.

He wasn't a tagalong kid brother. He was just always sort of . . . there. He had his life and I had mine. They rarely intersected.

Until Notre Dame.

The problem with choosing to root for a team from South

Bend, Indiana, when you live in Toronto, Canada, is that you have no one to impress with your knowledge. What's the point of committing to memory a detailed biography of Ara Parseghian (b. Akron, Ohio; briefly a member of the Cleveland Browns) if no one knows or cares that you did it?

Brendan became that person. Without prompting, he read the same books and learned the same obscure trivia and, honestly, was better at it than I was.

We would trade *Blue & Gold* between us and have long, deep discussions about the seventeen-year-olds who'd just committed to Notre Dame. We had intense opinions about whether four defensive linemen was too many in the freshman class, if it came at the expense of the receiving corps.

We knew the names of these kids, their stats, how they were doing in school. (In the ugly world of U.S. college athletics, Notre Dame handicapped itself by insisting its student-athletes actually pass their classes. The team was often critically short of big, stupid people.) We knew which states produced the best players at specific positions. We knew which high-school programs mattered in Florida and Texas.

If we had applied a fraction of this passion for learning to our day jobs, we'd both be nuclear physicists. Instead, we can tell you a lot about Lou Holtz's tactical devotion to the read-option.

It made sense at the time.

We'd missed the high point. Notre Dame won a national championship in 1988. We came in the next fall, fresh to the fight and ready for more. It wouldn't work out.

We started to watch the games together on Saturday afternoons. I bought Brendan a shirt. We would sit in front of the television and scream at it—evoking shades of my early childhood and Mickey Hamill. It was glorious. We were together and of one mind.

The tribe I'd found at school on the football team was replaced by the smaller, more important one I'd discovered at home. I'd always loved Brendan. That sense of mutual responsibility for the other's well-being was drilled into us by our mother. But now we had something to talk about, and I realized I liked him.

For men who do not know each other or have much in common, sports is a shared language.

I am not going to belly up to a hotel bar in Savannah, Georgia, and begin talking politics with the stranger sitting next to me. That won't end well. But if there's a game on, that's an invitation. You watch for a while. One of you says, "Nice catch." The other nods. You spin off to a game you saw the other day or something you heard about a trade. If you have a basis of sports knowledge—very little will do the trick—it's an endless well of conversational foreplay.

A couple of years after Brendan and I had found this common ground, I moved away for school. I came home to work in the summers, but those reunions were awkward. He was changing. The lightness in him was giving way to something more shopworn and dented by life. He was becoming a man. I didn't know about the daily goings-on in his life. I was consumed by the minutiae of my own.

After two more years, I came home to go to school and moved in with my girlfriend. I'd come to the house to use the washer/dryer on the weekends. If Brendan was around, we'd talk about Notre Dame, but he wasn't around that much.

But I reassured myself that we still had this connection. I'd tell him we should go to a bar and watch the game. Not this weekend. I was busy this weekend. But maybe next?

The next never came.

Since he was less fickle in his loves, Brendan maintained his loyalty to the Irish—he still watched every game, he still wore a sweatshirt I'd gotten him in Indiana, made a point of putting it on when I came over. But my own was flagging. I couldn't bring myself to keep up with the goings-on, the new recruits, the gossip. There was too much of it and it felt like work. I wanted to read about other things.

My girlfriend's older brother, Bobby, was a Florida State fan. In the early nineties, that program was on the rise, while Notre Dame's was in descent. We went over to her parents' house to watch a bowl game at New Year's. That family was everything my own was not—large, moneyed, tight-knit. They were a Rockwell painting. I envied their ease in the world. They knew they belonged.

Florida State and Notre Dame played each other in that game. It went badly for my side. I'd had a few drinks and was in foul humour. Ruthless teasing is central to a good sports friendship, but I was in no mood. Bobby whooped at every play.

I started to swear theatrically, knowing it would offend the room.

Eventually, my girlfriend's father said tightly, "Mrs. Haggert doesn't like that sort of language."

"Then Mrs. Haggert can tell me herself."

It was a churlish thing to do. That's why I did it. My girlfriend was eyeing me with mounting horror.

The game turned on one play. I don't remember the play. I remember bringing my fist down so hard on the coffee table that it cracked.

For a surreal moment, there was the genuine possibility of a fist fight. You could feel that. The women—my girlfriend, her mother, her sister—rose instinctively from their seats and moved into the centre of the room. Blocking the path. Obscuring the sightlines. Once you can't see someone's eyes, your rage fades. The moment passed.

We left quickly. My girlfriend was furious. After four years, that relationship was coming apart. This was a symptom.

I didn't apologize, but I was humiliated.

After that, rooting for Notre Dame stopped making sense to me. I'd used that team as camouflage to fit in. I didn't need it anymore. And just like that, I stopped paying attention. Today, I couldn't tell you who coaches the team, how they're doing or where they finished last year. I couldn't name a single player from the past decade off the top of my head.

Brendan and I are middle-aged men now. When we get together for a coffee or a drink, one of the first things he'll say is, "Did you see the Notre Dame game?"

And I lie.

THE CHURCH

WHEN SHE WAS A GIRL IN RURAL IRELAND, my mother's family went to church on Sundays as a community obligation and on sufferance. It was three miles by horse and buggy. The neighbours, most of them farmers, had built their own house of worship. It didn't bear a saint's name. It marked the nearest village—Renanirree Church.

They brought in a priest named Father Murphy from a nearby parish to mind God's business. In Ireland in the fifties, one parish over might as well have been an ocean away. People did not warm to this pushy foreigner—but they dared not say anything about it.

At the time, the Catholic Church in Ireland was more of a shakedown operation/guilt factory than a place of sacred healing. You paid for your family pew. Where you sat said a great deal about your social standing. In order to goose donations and discourage thrift, the weekly offerings were read aloud during the service—"John Buckley, seven (shillings) and six (pence)" and so forth.

To make the sermons relatable, Father Murphy framed them around whatever was happening in the village. Who'd gotten pregnant out of wedlock, for example. No names were used because, in a parish of just a few dozen families, none were required—everyone already knew what was what. But this was an opportunity to sit through an excruciating rhetorical stoning in what passed for the public square.

Some of the village men didn't embrace Father Murphy's take on community relations. They'd linger outside as mass began, watching the women pass and gossiping amongst themselves. This was a non-starter. If anyone was missing at the outset, Father Murphy would rush out and harangue them into the building. If that didn't work, he would take bodily hold of objectors and throw them into the church. He was a sort of bouncer in reverse and, by the sounds of it, a terror.

A significant part of Father Murphy's influence stemmed from the local belief that he had both the ability and the inclination to curse people. Not just wish you ill or rubbish your good name, but actually cast a metaphysical hex that would bring very tangible disaster to your life.

My grandfather lived in fear that he would run afoul of Father Murphy and have the evil eye turned in his direction so that his crops would fail or his cattle would die or someone in the family would get sick. My grandfather also believed that if you built a house at a crossroads, anyone who stayed there overnight would perish. And that his own mother had heard the banshee—another portent of death—just days before an itinerant salesman showed up unannounced at the farm, walked into the barn and dropped dead.

But the church was the focus of his dread.

Whenever my mother or her siblings misbehaved, they were reminded of this awesome and capricious power that lay in wait only three miles away, watching them. My grandfather was not one of the men who refused to take his seat on Sunday morning.

As he aged, his faith intensified. Whatever he'd been afraid of during the prime of his life consumed him as he neared the end.

In the best tradition of Irish miserabilism, this all sounds vaguely charming now. But it doesn't explain why they did it at the time. "Why would you put yourself through this?" I once asked my mother.

"Going to church is good for you," she said. "You have to get up. You have to make yourself presentable. You have to talk to your neighbours."

That makes sense, though I don't remember it sounding that reasonable when I was a kid. I do recall the obligation part. Ours was not a household in which the art of explaining was much practised. Things happened, and you accepted them. My mother brought that much over from County Cork.

As a child, it would not have occurred to me to resent going to church. I can't say how it goes down in other religions, but most Catholic indoctrination is a function of rote learning. You memorize and repeat the words. Your lizard brain does all the work. That was 90 percent of how I worshipped, and I did it happily. I enjoyed the rigour, things happening in a set and unchanging order. The key to unlocking the rhythms of life is figuring out the patterns—when I do this, this subsequent thing happens. Later, you'll begin fiddling with the order, trying to break up the monotony of existence. But when you're a kid, it's hard enough trying to keep everything straight.

Church was easy that way. Sit, stand, kneel. Sit, stand, kneel. I didn't enjoy the kneeling. Even as an eight-year-old, some part of you understands that supplication diminishes you. And it is difficult to get comfortable on a knobby wooden kneeler. I still recall my mother's head turning whenever I tried to lean back and rest my ass on the bench. She'd lay those Manson lamps on me and I'd lurch back to vertical. No sloth in church.

But I always liked a day out and the feeling of going to our church to sit in our pew and listen to our priest. It's the last vestige of tribalism and, if you turn it a certain way, true ownership.

As a high-school kid, that changed. I would like to say that I chafed at the authoritarianism, but really I just wanted to sleep in on Sundays. I did try the tack of moral outrage. But as a not-terribly-devout devout Catholic, my mother was able to deploy a logical jiu-jitsu that no amount of teenage angst could overpower.

"But don't you think that there should be women priests?"

"Yes, there certainly should."

"Then doesn't that mean we're supporting a corrupt organization?"

"Yes, probably. But you're still going."

So I went.

My mother and younger brother would go Saturday nights, when I was busy drinking with friends or at work. I went alone the next morning.

Our priest at St. Cecilia's, Father Manley, did a nice, quick mass—a half-hour start to finish. The sermon often amounted to something along the lines of "Well, what is Matthew trying to say here? Who's to say?" He believed in mysteries and the result was what an uncle of mine called "the McDonald's of Catholicism."

Though short, his mass was not short enough for me.

I'd heard somewhere that you had not technically missed the sacrament if you were present for the beginning of the blessing of gifts—where the bread and wine are turned into the metaphorical body and blood of Christ. Was this true? No way of knowing. Pre-internet, rumours were facts as long as you repeated them often enough. (And, come to think of it, post-internet as well.)

This holy wrinkle bought me ten extra minutes in bed while the suckers sat through the prelims.

On one awful occasion, I fell out of bed at the last moment, felt around half-blind on the floor for something to wear, pulled it on like a slug tugging on a body sock and left the house without looking down. On that day, I schlepped out of the house—I was fifteen—hungover and truly careless. I got on the bus. I got a couple of looks, but as my teenage hairstyles got weirder, I had gotten used to the looks.

My routine was to enter the church quietly, then stand in the foyer at the back rather than sit down. I would watch the proceedings through a doorway. There were always a couple of stragglers back there. After twenty minutes of boredom, I'd walk up to receive the host, swing back up the aisle and march out of the building. If things played out right, there'd be a westbound bus pulling up across the street as I exited.

When I got there that day, an older lady I did not recognize was also standing in the back. She gave me a look. And the look did not end. She openly gawped at me.

I gave her an appraising glance in return. That usually worked. No effect.

I turned away for a couple of seconds, then turned back. Still staring.

I escalated things—raised eyebrow and slight sneer. Still staring.

Finally, I threw out my hands—"What?"

She pointed at me. I looked down.

Oh.

I was in the midst of a pitiable phase of wearing nothing but rock t-shirts. The one I now had on inside the house of God was a reprint of a Dead Kennedys album cover. It featured a chalk outline of a body with the screaming caption "Too Drunk to Fuck."

I am trying to imagine something more offensive I might have put on for a pleasant Sunday morning of worship. Maybe a belt of human skulls. Or the words "I AM HERE TO KILL" smeared across my bare chest in pig's blood. But it's hard to get there. This was pretty irredeemable. If you have any doubt, read the lyrics.

What would Father Murphy have done? Beaten me to death with a crucifix in front of a cheering mob, probably. I can't say he'd have been wrong.

In the moment, the best I could think to do was misdirection. I pulled the shirt away from my body and regarded it thought-fully, trying to pantomime mild surprise—"Oh jeepers, how did this get on me?"

The lady wasn't buying it. She bugged her eyes out and ges-tured toward the door with her head. I looked back, caught somewhere between petulance and humiliation.

Had I my wits about me, I might have gone to the bathroom in the basement and turned the shirt inside out. But I have not been gifted with many wits and didn't want to have gone to the trouble of having gone to church without having officially gone to church. More importantly, I didn't want to give her the satisfaction. So that meant I'd have to make the long walk up to the front.

I stood there for another fifteen minutes, angling the front of my body away from the view of passersby. I could have folded my arms across my chest, but that seemed too much like submission.

The lady continued to helpfully stare, her alarm settling into disgust. Which meant I was winning. I pictured her going home later: "How was church?" "Uneventful. Wait, there was one thing. I stood beside the Antichrist." The time eventually came to go up and receive the sacrament from Father Manley. I waited for the lady to go first, lest she try to rip the shirt off me as I entered the church proper.

St. Cecilia's was never quite full. There were perhaps two hundred people there that day. I folded myself into line, pressed up hard against the man directly in front of me. I repeatedly tripped over his heels as he sighed with increasing irritation. Everyone was facing forward, obscuring my apostasy.

Only Father Manley could properly see me. He had the priestly habit of giving everyone a good hard look as he said, "The body of Christ," then pausing for a long beat after you responded with "Amen."

Of course—of course, of course, of course—he spotted the shirt straight off. The cup held up chest-high dropped slowly as he read it to himself a few times. His face slackened and his eyelids fluttered. This was beginning to feel like a miscalculation.

He looked at me. I looked at him. He shook his head very slightly. I was too stubborn to feel genuine shame, but I did feel awfully stupid. He said his words, and I said mine back.

It is part of the ritual that once you have received the host, you leave with your hands clasped. I held mine in front of me and double-stepped toward the door.

On the way back into the house, I met my mother at the door. She looked at the shirt, then at me.

"Did you wear that to church?"

No point in lying—"Yes."

"You must have been quite a hit."

She pretended to be disappointed, but I know she was pleased. I often suspected that the only reason my mother continued to practise was that it gave her the moral standing to resent certain parts of the Church.

We didn't discuss religion in my house. It wasn't an off-limits topic, but it seemed too monolithic to bother mentioning. There was the Church and you went and that was it. In the south of Ireland even more so than the rest of the country, the institution was wrapped in romantic ideas about freedom and self-determination. The Church was an extension of the need to assert yourself.

For my mother, going to mass was a small act of rebellion—submitting to one authority in order to defy another. She still goes to church. I do not.

Shortly after the Great T-Shirt Debacle, I found the only excuse that trumped religious duty in my mother's calculus: a job. Neither my Saturday nights nor my Sunday mornings were free anymore. It is remarkable how something that accounts for such a regular part of your life can fade so quickly.

Now out of the habit, I return less than a half-dozen times a year—Good Friday, Easter Sunday, Christmas Eve and one or two furtive visits to confession. I am fairly certain there is no heaven or hell, but I'm not taking any chances. As such, I lack the courage to accept what Sartre called "the divine irresponsibility of the condemned man." I've become one of those Catholics.

Intermittently, this causes me guilt. Not because I've let down my mother or the Church or God. All three have more important things to worry about. But guilty because I've let a cornerstone of my identity slip from my grasp and replaced it with nothing. That thought most often occurs to me around Easter, beginning the first time I pass someone on Ash Wednesday with the telltale smudge of devotion pressed onto their forehead.

ANOTHER OF THE TRICKS of childhood is the illusion of permanence. "I will always live in this house with these people, go to this school and like this show and wear these shoes." One by one, those things are taken from you. You change schools, move house, find new things to like and different people. For a while, growth—any sort—is a thrill. But eventually it occurs to you that whatever you have now will be taken from you in due time.

That's another threshold of adulthood—the realization that life is not one long process. It's many short ones, punctuated at each break by loss. Maybe things will get better for you—you'll lose one thing to gain another that is preferable. But maybe not.

When alarmists talk about the extended adolescence of a generation (and I've now lived long enough to see it happen to several generations), they presume people are hiding from the responsibilities of adulthood. That's not it. They're trying to put off change. Very few people change willingly. They have to be forced into it by events.

The church (any sort of church) is a hedge against this fear. Yes, you may now have a new job, and a new wife, and new debts, but church hasn't changed. That continuum is as it was—live right, die happy, enjoy the fruits. That's a ninety-year plan that will not be interrupted by a mid-life crisis.

I gave that up, which, in retrospect, was foolish.

Though I did not recognize it as such at the time, there was a profound comfort in church. It wasn't the message or the teachings—though those remain a bulwark of civilization. It was something even greater.

I'm sure my Catholicism—or my grandfather's or my mother's—is not entirely like any other person's. It's possible it's not even close. I've always been curious about how other people, not just Catholics, pray. What do they say? How do they feel as they do it? Is there real communion with God? Is that possible?

Once you start down that mental path, the world falls away. Your trivial concerns, your problems, your faults, your secret desires—they all become insignificant as you consider the purpose, direction and meaning of human existence.

I remain convinced that we all confront that in church and that it is depressingly possible to avoid it everywhere else. Perhaps even likely. In church, this doesn't require discussion. I've never heard a sermon that changed my mind on any particular issue. The implicit bargain of worship is that you spend some time each week sitting still and giving thought to what it's all about.

You could do that at home, but you probably won't. There isn't time—you have too many photographs to like on Facebook.

When you go out to do this, there are other people to do it with you. You may not know them but you feel fairly certain you have something basic in common. You can assume you are all like-minded about at least one thing, have come together in goodwill and want to share an idea.

When I was not yet an idiotic middle-aged man but rather an idiotic teenager with a mohawk, earrings and an air of erratic aggression, strangers still wanted to shake my hand in church. Regardless of how I looked, they assumed we were on the same page. And though I might not have agreed at the time, I know now they were right.

That involved more than accepting that Jesus was a real person and that he rose on the third day. It was more profound than that.

I cannot assume when I walk into any home, bar, shop or other place of business that I will receive a warm welcome. One would like to think so, but one can't know. We've all experienced that small feeling of doubt before we cross certain thresholds— "Do I belong here?" I have never felt I belonged anywhere. I have had moments where I felt things were going right in the world and that I was part of that. But belonged? That assumes too much. I am here in the world, but I am a visitor (not even a guest). It has never been in me to join anything.

Church was a small respite from that feeling. I assume that all people of good intent will be embraced in any church, any mosque, any synagogue or any temple. Because if that were not the case, there would be no reason for those places to exist. I also assume that's why people do it. You get up. You make yourself presentable. You talk to your neighbours. God is the reason they built the place, but community is the reason people go. That's the heart of it.

I suspect I'll end up back at church someday. More than any deep spiritual longing, it's too perfect an arc.

Because even if you leave the church and do not return, church never really leaves you.

LISTS

THE ONLY GIFTS I REMEMBER RECEIVING as a child were ones given by my father, largely because he had the habit of giving you things he wanted for himself. You'd get books you couldn't yet read, or clothes that fit him rather than you or something bizarre you knew he'd bought on a whim after several rum and Cokes.

He was Fred Flintstone, giving his wife a bowling ball when she was hoping for a fur coat.

One Christmas he gave Brendan a stuffed crocheted chicken. As a general rule, eight-year-olds don't like things that are stuffed or crocheted or chickens. The only way this thing could have been a more inappropriate present for a child was if my father had lit it on fire before entering the house.

My brother was an eerily poised child. He unwrapped the chicken, took a good look at it, put it down and left the room. My father was not pleased. That was another of his things—get you something he knew you wouldn't like, and then sulk when you didn't like it.

He'd done some dumb child-gifting before—a set of Ukrainian nesting dolls also stands out—but this was a special effort. That chicken wasn't just useless. It was also remarkably ugly—enormous and rust-coloured. It was stitched together from wool so coarse you could have used that chicken to sand a deck. It had little black beads for eyes. They rolled around inside translucent orbs so that that chicken was always staring directly at you when you entered a room. It was the sort of chicken you expected to wake up and find sitting on your chest late at night, holding an ice pick.

We moved several times during my childhood. During each switch, Brendan and I would lose half our stuff. But not that chicken. Six days or six weeks or six months after a move, he'd pop up on a shelf, like it had taken him that long to track us down.

A while back, I asked my brother if he still had the chicken. He said no.

And I thought, "Great. That chicken is still out there. Stalking me."

But to that chicken's credit, it stood out from the mountain of detritus one collects in childhood.

I had toys. I'm sure of that. I can't remember any of them specifically unless I consult a listicle of "Popular Toys of the '70s." There were G.I. Joes and *Stars Wars* figures. There must have been a Slinky and a Stretch Armstrong. I had a four-foot-high stuffed cat that I'd won by cheating in a colouring contest at the local drug store (my father did it for me).

The only birthday or Christmas present I can still recall using was a large volume entitled *The Big Book of Lists* given to me by an aunt and uncle. There were hundreds of random entries:

"Ten Tallest Buildings"; "Seven Wonders of the World"; "Largest Capital Cities."

I tried to memorize each one for later deployment in casual conversation: "It's a funny thing you mention aqueducts. Are you familiar with the six longest in the world? I'll give you Rome and then you can guess the others."

I made my own lists—places I'd been, how many people I knew, jobs I wanted, a ranking of school subjects. I thought of everything I encountered in list format. Where did the movie I'd just watched rank all time? Or the TV show?

Into my late twenties, I carried around a series of diaries listing every book I'd ever read—how many pages it contained, when it had been started and finished, and a mark out of five stars. I loved reading, but I got a special thrill from being able to pad the list.

Life is not orderly, but a list can make it so. As you change, so do your lists.

I no longer believe that *The Breakfast Club* is one of the ten best films ever made. But there was a younger version of myself who did. An astrophysicist once told me, "You cannot properly consider a system of which you are a part." (It's one of the Top 20 Aphorisms I've Encountered in Conversation.)

So while I remember the iteration of myself who thought Molly Ringwald dancing on a staircase and Emilio Estevez talking about ripping the hair off some guy's ass was right up there with *La Règle du Jeu*, I'm not sure I would recognize him now.

However, I can make certain assumptions about him because I have the list as a reference point. If the list is long enough, you can make good guesses about someone's personality and approach. You can tell if this is someone you'd like.

In journalism, lists are considered the lowest form of literature, tucked in behind streeters and notes columns. A list is what you print in August when everyone's on vacation and you can't come up with anything better.

I've never understood that pervasive opinion. I defy you to read past a list on a printed page. It's impossible. Because you know that while ten thousand words of explication may tell you nothing about the author, a list can't help but do so. It lets you flip through the filing system of someone's brain. It's a form of mind reading.

It's my book so I get to inflict just a few of my lists on you.

I apologize in advance if they do not offend you. That was my intention. I'll try to learn from this and do better in future.

UNDERRATED FILM CLASSICS

1. *Sorcerer*
2. *Alien 3*
3. *Weird Science*
4. *Tremors*
5. *The Hit* (1984)
6. *The Long Good Friday*
7. *Fail Safe*
8. *Antonia's Line*
9. *Layer Cake*
10. *Sneakers* (1992)

GOOD THINGS THAT NO LONGER EXIST

1. Being unreachable
2. Ignorance of the daily news cycle
3. Rotary dial
4. Remembering phone numbers
5. Silence
6. Darkness
7. Smoking on subway platforms
8. Music videos as destination television
9. Aerosol deodorant

BOOKS YOU WANTED TO BE THE SORT OF PERSON
WHO LIKED, BUT COULD NOT GET THERE

1. Dante's *Inferno*
2. *Moby Dick*
3. *On the Road*
4. *The Catcher in the Rye*
5. *Ulysses*
6. *War and Peace*
7. *Middlemarch*
8. *The Alexandria Quartet*
9. *To the Lighthouse*
10. *The Bell Jar*

WORST PLACES

1. The middle seat
2. Cleveland after dark
3. Disney World/Land
4. Cleveland in daylight
5. Any hotel room facing a highway
6. O'Hare Airport at Christmas
7. A twenty-four-hour coffee shop between 2 and 5 a.m.
8. The front row at a movie theatre
9. Any lineup for any reason
10. Budapest

GREAT NOVELS ABOUT BASEBALL

1. *The Natural*—Malamud
   There is no number two.

GOOD BOOKS ABOUT THE VIETNAM WAR

1. *A Bright Shining Lie*—Sheehan
2. *Dispatches*—Herr
3. *The Things They Carried*—O'Brien
4. *In Pharaoh's Army*—Wolff
5. *A Rumor of War*—Caputo
6. *The Quiet American*—Greene

OVERRATED EXPERIENCES

1. Picnics
2. Being there
3. Concerts in arenas
4. Canoeing
5. The Louvre
6. Theatre in a park
7. Cross-country skiing
8. Opening night
9. Pop-up anything
10. Cooking over an open fire

TEN COMPELLING COMICS BEFORE ANTI-HEROES,
CROSSOVERS AND IRONY RUINED EVERYTHING

1. *The New Mutants*
2. *Conan the Barbarian*
3. *Shang-Chi: Master of Kung Fu*
4. *Archie*
5. *The Amazing Spider-Man*
6. *Alpha Flight*
7. *X-Men* (before it got stupid)
8. *Lone Wolf and Cub*
9. *Daredevil* (Frank Miller era)
10. *Longshot*

SONGS FROM *FOOTLOOSE*, RANKED

1. "Almost Paradise"
2. "Holding Out for a Hero"
3. "I'm Free"
4. "Dancing in the Sheets"
5. "Let's Hear It for the Boy"
6. "Somebody's Eyes"
7. "Footloose"
8. "Never"
9. "The Girl Gets Around"

BEST UNIFORMS

1. Notre Dame
2. Brazilian national football team
3. Montreal Canadiens
4. New York Yankees
5. Penn State
6. Toronto Maple Leafs
7. FC Barcelona
8. Boston Red Sox
9. Italian national football team
10. Chicago Blackhawks

MARTIN SCORSESE'S FEATURE FILMS, RANKED

1. *Goodfellas*
2. *Raging Bull*
3. *The Wolf of Wall Street*
4. *The King of Comedy*
5. *Mean Streets*
6. *Casino*
7. *The Departed*
8. *Taxi Driver*
9. *The Age of Innocence*
10. *Cape Fear*
24. *After Hours*

MOST EFFECTIVE EXCUSES

1. None. Nobody cares about your excuses.
2. "I apologize unreservedly."
3. "Is that really what you wanted?"
4. "This is news to me."
5. "Are you sure you gave it to me?"
6. "They didn't have it."
7. "What can I tell you?"
8. "I feel like I did that already."
9. "That's not what he told me."
10. "I think you've got it backwards."

CITIES, RANKED

1. New York
2. London
3. Berlin
4. Prague
5. Florence
6. Nairobi
7. Vienna
8. Johannesburg
9. Zagreb
10. Minneapolis

BEST BOOKS ABOUT NAZIS

1. *Inside the Third Reich*—Speer
2. *The Rise and Fall of the Third Reich*—Shirer
3. *Survival in Auschwitz*—Levi
4. *Hitler, 1936–45: Nemesis*—Kershaw
5. *SS-GB*—Deighton
6. *The Man in the High Castle*—Dick
7. *Albert Speer: His Battle with Truth*—Sereny
8. *Fatherland*—Harris
9. *Night*—Wiesel
10. *The Day After Tomorrow*—Folsom

ORWELL

THERE WAS A FIVE-YEAR WINDOW in the late eighties/
early nineties when getting a tattoo was still cool. Few people
had them at the time and those who did were the right sort of
people—bikers, hookers, seamen and other attractive degenerates. Tattoos were still rare enough that when you saw one, you
remarked on it. You read what it said and backed up a bit. It was
vaguely dangerous.

By the mid-nineties, that was over. Lower-back and ankle
tattoos had become an aspirational middle-class birthmark.
Your cool aunt wanted one. Tattoos on the face became the only
way those who planned a career in the penal system could get
any credibility from the exercise.

But back in that golden window of tattoo glory, I'd made
myself an expansive tattoo plan. First, I was going to get one on
my head. Above the ear, maybe. I was partial to the Public Enemy
symbol—the profile of a man in the crosshairs of a rifle sight. I'd
also designed a symbol of my own for an as-yet-unrealized street
gang I hoped to found called The Lunatic Fringe, which at

fifteen I thought quite clever. I've never had much of a visual imagination. The symbol was a stylized *L* superimposed over an *F* and was almost indistinguishable from a swastika.

If the proto-swastika on my head turned out to be a bad decision, there was an easy solution: I'd just grow my hair back over it. Presto whammo. Had that truly stupid idea worked out, I'm not sure how my life would have gone as an ersatz Heinrich Himmler with male pattern baldness. But thankfully when I was fifteen tattoos were expensive and hard to get; and I was poor and had no follow-through.

My second tattoo vision was a five-man plan. Sort of like Shazam and the Roman gods who seeded his power, I would carve upon me the five men who informed my world view.

I suppose it says something about the unfinished nature of that foundational personal philosophy that I've forgotten two of them. I hope to Christ neither was a professional wrestler. The first guy was the Irish rebel and martyr Michael Collins. The second was Malcolm X (I'd just read his autobiography and its finishing touches on inclusion and human solidarity had felt very profound to me). Collins and X were late discoveries, relatively speaking. They'd come to me as a generalized teenage purposelessness and rage began searching for some useful, bookish conduit. I'd eventually end up at Frantz Fanon and Bolshevism, but before I could go all little-red-book I got too busy working for a living. This is why all personal revolutions end—because you have a double shift on Saturday.

My third tattoo man had been with me much longer—George Orwell.

For a certain sort of person, there is a lifelong struggle between those writers and books you claim to like best versus those you actually do. Most of what we read is literary corn syrup—easily digestible and runs right through us. Cheap mysteries, borderline pornography, John Grisham, stories about precocious teenagers with telepathy hunting each other in the near future—that's the bulk of our diet.

We don't sit down to absorb these books so much as graze on them while doing other things—riding the subway or burning time in a waiting room.

"Real" literary time is spent in a comfortable chair and booked in advance. You might make yourself a cup of tea and cross your legs like you once saw William Buckley do. You are Reading. It requires concentration. You are *growing as a person*. You can feel it. Is your head expanding? Quite possibly!

After a while you grow bored, but you hold on to the *feeling* proper literature gives. And you tell other people about it. That's important. There is no point reading a *good* book unless others have heard—or better yet, seen—that you've done so.

Orwell closed this loop. He was a great writer, great thinker and great entertainer. He is, to my mind, the most usefully instructional writer in English—spare language; staccato sentences; propositions instead of meanders; the chronological arrangement of narrative. If you want to know how to write well, copy Orwell as best you can.

And, like few major authors in history, his collected work was tiered to hit you at key moments in the development of your interior life.

I started out with *Animal Farm* as a grade-schooler. I was alerted to the fact that this book was special because my mother insisted on reading it to us. As a rule, she did not do a "bedtime routine." There was no "tucking in," no petting back the hair, no staring into our eyes and telling us how precious we were. There was a steady escalation of threats that started around eight and ended near ten with shouting and lights shut off, followed by surprise guerrilla forays into the room to see if any of the natives were still active past curfew.

This went on for years and years because my mother had a farmer's fixation on when people should and should not be asleep. In the day? Absolutely not. Not unless you'd just come out of surgery, and even then. At night? Absolutely. And no half-assed stuff—no nightlights, no music in the background. Curtains pulled, blankets at chin, unconscious for eight solid hours. She'd have drugged us if it had occurred to her. And then it all started again. This military precision has blessed/cursed me since. I am incapable of sleeping in without feeling an enormous weight of guilt (and I do so constantly, which means the dysfunctional snake has truly swallowed its tail).

So on the night she announced that bedtime would be delayed and literature would be read aloud, it seemed a trap. What was going on here? Was all my stuff going to be removed while I was distracted? Would strangers annex the living room? Was this all a pretext to calamity?

Fair to say that I first came to Orwell primed with the proper, paranoid mindset. *Animal Farm* is not a long book. It runs, like the best stories, in order. It is chilling but emotionally detached. There's no simpering or pandering—the worst parts of all children's literature. Some of the best advice I've received on writing is that it is finished once you have held it up and shaken out all the extra words. *Animal Farm* had no extra words.

Thinly veiled, the book is the Russian Revolution channelled through Old MacDonald. The animals on a farm revolt. They send the humans to flight. Led by two pigs, Snowball and Napoleon, they create a socialist nirvana. And then things start to slide.

The allegory here penetrable by the mind of a child but subtle enough to appeal to adults. It's premised on two basic features of life you must understand to survive—nothing is fair; and everyone is a hypocrite when it suits them.

Are you going to be a Napoleon or a Snowball? Are you going to be the revolutionary who wins or the one who will not go the whole way? Seriously, who would want to be a Snowball in this scenario? It's a fat blob of nothingness that melts as soon as matters heat up. With necessary amendments, I'll be the guy up on my hind legs, thanks very much.

Worse, you could be a Boxer and get marched off to the glue factory on the basis of your principles. Boxer—the horse—was the hero of every other book I'd read to that point, and here he was a schlemiel who cannot feel the direction of the wind changing.

The book doesn't get really grim until the last few pages and then it just ends. The force coming from the implied final act— "Things got much worse for all involved and then continued on like that, forever." This literary device was new and exciting—a book you are meant to *imagine* to its finale. It was my first experience of post-modernism.

My mother and I did not discuss our feelings about the book afterward. It was left to me to read it again at my leisure. We were not a didactic family in that way, which is why my mother's Bolshie politics never fully infected my own. Caring only that I had the critical information, and not caring how I interpreted it, was one of her gifts to me. She was a true anti-authoritarian. She didn't feel the need to convince you of anything or turn you to her way of thinking. These days that would make her as rare as a fucking dodo.

Were you going to be the person screwing people over in life or the one getting screwed? *Animal Farm* was a sort of Nietzschean primer on this question. Given his own first-hand experience with political utopianism—he got shot in the neck for his trouble—Orwell offered no middle ground on this score. There was no third way that allowed you to save your skin as well as your pride. This was pure "one-or-the-other"-ism. Even as a nine- or ten-year-old, I appreciated the dull honesty.

As I suppose my mother had intended, *Animal Farm* awakened in me an early mistrust of systems and their rewards. My own solution to the choice between tyrant and victim was to opt out. I would be the person who did not adopt philosophies or sign on to political modes of thought. I'd be the distant cynic, the person narrating the tragedy of existence from a safe remove. In essence, I'd be Orwell himself. I'm not sure this was his point, but it was the point I took. I would not become a writer for a long time. But though it did not occur to me then, this was the beginning of that urge.

Of course, as a child you don't think of it in this organized a way—"I am a dissenter in the Greek tradition, and will, when asked, drink the hemlock without ever having bent"—but Orwell made it easy to apply his own rules to the observed reality of the schoolyard. You knew who the pigs were, and realized distressingly that you were probably a sheep. There was only one honourable way out of that bind. *Animal Farm* gave you the road map.

Orwell popped into my consciousness a second time in 1984, when I was turning twelve, and "Did he call it right?" became a pop culture sensation. A lot of people seemed to believe that Winston Smith's rise-and-shine calisthenics while being shouted at by the interactive view screen presaged the *20 Minute Workout*, as if that was what Orwell had been after—knocking off H.G. Wells.

Most failed then to notice (and still do) that *1984* was not a work of prediction or a warning. Instead, it was a piece of journalism relevant to all eras. It referred most precisely to the way in which free people organize their own intellectual confinement.

This time the allegory was subtler, and perhaps only perceptible to children, since they had not yet been invested in the game. All of us want to be fooled. Orwell wasn't showing us how to avoid that. He was only reminding us of the fact.

What struck me most about that book was the nobility of a doomed resistance. Doomed being the operative difference from every other piece of art I imbibed.

Winston was always going to be crushed by the system. You knew that from page one. The only possible redemption was in doing it on his own terms. He doesn't manage it. He fails himself and the only person he cares about. In the end, he survives. He can't even manage to become a Boxer.

What a freeing idea. That there is a real possibility life *will not work out the way you'd hoped*. That you will become less than you imagined. Perhaps even much less.

At the time, there was a pedagogic rage for aptitude tests. We were forever filling out forms designed to tell us "what we were meant to be." There was a strong tendency toward wish fulfillment in all this. Indiana Jones was a big thing at the time and I thought I'd like to be that—a swashbuckling archaeologist. We even had a whip that my brother would take out intermittently so we could flay each other.

Of course, that profession popped up a lot in my tests—archaeologist.

Like that was ever going to happen.

I knew in my bones that I was going to be an archaeologist like I was going to be the principal in a production of *La Cage aux Folles*. I could pirouette around the living room all I liked, but it wasn't going to change the fact that I was a clumsy oaf.

What these aptitude tests never told you was that you were bound to be a mid-level cipher in the IT department of some insurance company. Which was far more likely.

You may not fail in life, but the odds that you would succeed in the way they kept telling you was possible in school were so remote as to be statistically insignificant. No one had the courage to tell you that. Most teachers were by definition people who'd pulled up short on their aspirations—why teach science or drama rather than be a scientist or an actor?—though they hadn't the salt to explain to you that that was how things worked.

Our high-school football coach once told us, with a straight face no less, that if we really worked at it—hit the gym early, listened carefully, lived right—any one of us could play pro football. Maybe not in the NFL, but Canadian football for sure.

We were all down on a knee at the time, getting the old pep talk after a game. A lot of kids in the room had this "Really?" look, as if they believed what he was saying. Several faces had a moony, dream-a-little-dream cast, as if they were making a decision. I was looking a little lower, at their chubby/scrawny/averagely sized teenage bodies, thinking a different sort of "Really?" Like, really? REALLY?! Were we supposed to buy this nonsense?

This wasn't inspirational. It was a bald-faced lie. No one in this room was playing professional football unless they survived an overnight stay in a nuclear accelerator.

What he should have been doing was telling us to spend less time working out and more time force-feeding ourselves algebra. Get a job at McDonald's and start buying Apple stock. Invest 10 percent of your take-home pay. Marry someone you like who likes you. Don't be a jerk to people. It all comes around.

Most important of all, acclimate yourself to the idea that none of this will play out the way you think. Don't accept that you don't know. *Know* you don't know.

Teachers wouldn't tell you that, but George Orwell did. You will be an office drone. You will shuffle paper all day long and be alone at night. You will suffer quietly and, if lucky, take pleasure in small diversions. You will not be remarkable in any way. In the end, you will let yourself down. Life might not turn out quite so grim, but I thought it best to be prepared with that in mind. Better a pleasant surprise than a certain disappointment.

Which brought me to the third stage of Orwell—his reportage.

This worked in opposite order to Orwell's own life. He'd begun as an idealist and was disabused of his notions. The journalism was his first work. Though real, this writing was Orwell's true fantasy. That you could pack up and go to cover a war in Spain, then be so moved by what you saw there that you signed up to fight instead. Was that really possible? Apparently, since he'd done it.

Like most of the people I grew up with, we did not travel. A couple of sporadic trips back to Ireland that I can only barely recall. Once to Niagara Falls. Relatives in Northern Ontario. But there were no vacations, as such, no explorations abroad.

There wasn't the money to do so and there was no peer pressure, either. People stayed home. The schoolyard was our cottage. We paid taxes toward public pools and were goddamn well going to use them.

I didn't do much more than hang around, which seems in retrospect good preparation for life. That's what most of us spend our adulthood doing—accepting responsibilities no one has prepared us for and muddling through.

But here was a counter-example from an arch-cynic. Though he didn't seem to believe such a thing was possible—not if you were to judge him on the writing I was familiar with—Orwell had done something with himself. I absorbed these works—*Down and Out in Paris and London, The Road to Wigan Pier* and most especially *Homage to Catalonia*—as time travelogue and escapism. The politics were beside the point. I was bound up in the adventure of them. I perceived Orwell like I did all writers—as old—but his self-destructive enthusiasm shone through. In his middle thirties, he was the teenager I would have liked to have been.

Eventually, if you are lucky, as a child you will meet someone who can show you how to be a man. Not in the hagiographic "good person/full life/leave a legacy" sense. But how to cope.

I knew that my options in this regard were limited. I was never going to join anything. I couldn't be part of a movement, or sign on to a popular way of being. That wasn't in me. I was always going to be apart. Orwell was to me the type I might aspire to—the interested observer; the self-contained loner. He could be near great events without feeling the need to influence them. He found meaning in existing on the periphery.

Of course, this doesn't exactly jibe with hooking up with anarchists during the Spanish Civil War, but that isn't the point of *Homage to Catalonia*. His martial participation is cut short by a bullet wound. He spends most of the book in some stage of escape. Most of what he does in there is *see* things and tell you about them. He's just wandering around writing things down, not at all sure that any of it will be read.

But it all seemed to me purposeful. And more to the point, useful.

The most fascinating things about life are the banalities we so rarely discuss amongst ourselves but that we devote most of our energies to navigating. How did that day you've forgotten look? What did it feel like? Were you lonely? Did you have the sense you were progressing anywhere? Probably not. Yet string a few thousand of them together and that's a life.

Orwell had a particular gift for drawing deep impressions from shallow encounters. He could glance past someone—the unnamed Italian militiaman who opens *Homage*, for instance, the one he liked so much despite not speaking with nor ever seeing again—and make that person real to you.

This was to me true art. Not making something great seem so. That's easy. But finding something meaningless and giving it its due.

I was fourteen or fifteen years old and beginning to come to terms with the idea that nothing I would do would impact more than a few people. And that whatever impact I did create would not last.

The world fought me hard on this realization. It needed me to believe that this all had some ultimate purpose. Otherwise, I might give up on it and become a problem.

Over his short career (fifteen years or so before an untimely death) and in his roundabout way, Orwell taught me how bad the deal was. But also that you do not have to be in the system, nor do you have to exist outside it. All you need do is hang around the edges, watching. No one can force you out of something you don't have any desire to join. There is some hope for life's conscientious objectors.

And there is some happiness to be had in it. The less you depend on the big successes, the more you can enjoy those small diversions. It's all a matter of proportion and expectation.

It is a marvel to me that they are still banning Orwell's books. China just struck *1984* off the official list in 2018. But that fear misapprehends his true power, for me at least. Though he wrote about revolutions, Orwell wasn't trying to incite one. Rather the opposite. He told certain young readers that life was a phony war that always ended one way. Your only course is girding yourself for it. Whatever fight there is will be internal and, in the end, will have meaning only insofar as you provide it.

In other words, don't let other people decide for you. Decide for yourself.

I never did get that Orwell tattoo. And if I had, I'd have had to have it removed. It was the opposite of what I learned.

THE UMBRELLA

LOOKING BACK, I suspect that most of us know exactly when our childhoods ended. Assuming you weren't forcibly married in your teens to a village elder or feudal lord, this probably happened somewhere in your twenties. Or your thirties (smarten up). Or I suppose it could be your forties (though that is wrong and I pity your spouse).

The umbrella was my moment.

At age twenty-five, lacking a job, a girlfriend, an apartment and any prospects, I went to Belgium for the summer. I'd gone there after meeting a producer named Erik at a documentary film festival. Erik was my idea of what an auteur looked like—good hair, limpid blue eyes, a permanent expression of bemusement. Most impressively, he smoked like a movie Nazi—cigarette held between middle and ring finger.

We got blind drunk one evening in Toronto and I talked far too enthusiastically about Thomas Pynchon. (There is only one age at which it is permissible to talk about Thomas Pynchon at all—twenty-five—but you still sound like a pompous nitwit while doing so.) It all felt very artistic.

Erik asked me what I was doing with my life and I didn't have the good sense to be embarrassed or the presence of mind to lie. I was doing absolutely nothing. He invited me to spend a few months at his house. We'd do a movie together. No, really. He said that.

It didn't make much sense, but it felt very European—asking a complete stranger with no skills of any kind to come into the bosom of your family and potentially destroy your livelihood on the basis of one choppy filibuster about *Gravity's Rainbow*. I assumed this was how most things got done on the Continent.

I pointed out that I had absolutely no money and no chance of making any. I'd only just graduated from school with a use-less degree, been fired from my first real job, split up with my live-in girlfriend and landed penniless in my mother's half-finished basement. I'd fallen so far, so quickly that I was in the space beyond dignity. I was post-dignity.

So I laid the money problem on the table and waited for him to pick it up. Without hesitating—and in retrospect, this is the part I have trouble believing—he did. He was in the process of connecting one house to the adjacent one. He'd need some help with the construction work. Was I handy?

"Yes," I lied.

Well then, he'd pay me for that. Plus, he'd feed and house me for free.

Feeling more adrift than adventurous, and still quite drunk, I agreed.

Erik went back to Belgium. I went back to the basement and forgot all about it. A few weeks later, he emailed and repeated the offer. I'd spent most of the interim lying in bed staring at the faux log trim and feeling sorry for myself. I wasn't sure Belgium was a good idea, but it couldn't be any worse than this.

Since I had no money, I had to ask my mother for the airfare.

The Irish have many clichéd attributes, all of which are true. The one that doesn't get enough press is suspicion. This pathology is so pervasive that it's been rendered culturally inert—every Irishman and -woman believes that every other person is on the make, and comes to decisions accordingly. That way, everybody thinks they're the ones getting over on everyone else.

I remember my mother coming home from work one day in foul humour because the guy driving her bus had been singing.

"And that was a problem because . . . ?"

"Singing," she said, nodding seriously. "And what do you think he's got to be singing about?"

Shoulder shrug.

"Right."

When I explained the Erik situation to her, she gave me that same nod and said, "Sure, this isn't a gay thing, is it?"

"No, mom. I don't think he needs to import boyfriends from overseas. You should see him smoke."

Erik was married and had three young children. Telling my mother this didn't help things any. Now we'd entered a new paranoid realm of imaginary perversion.

Nonetheless, she gave me the money and I went.

I had many hopes for that summer, few of which came to pass. I thought I'd learn a new language. I didn't. I thought I'd spend a lot of time in cafés and write a book. I didn't. I thought I'd have affairs. I didn't. I thought I'd become cool. I absolutely did not.

The closest I'd come to that was one night out with another movie producer, Geert. We went to some filmmakers' haunt where Geert began telling people that I was a famous American scriptwriter and "*de schrijver van* Speed 2"—*Speed* having recently been a box-office hit.

By the early hours, we had a group of fascinated hipsters surrounding our table asking me what Steven Spielberg was really like.

"By tomorrow, I am the most famous producer in all of Belgium," Geert announced. We staggered back to his apartment. He put on the soundtrack to *Once Upon a Time in America*, stood swaying in the middle of his living room and cried. Then I drove home in the dark in a borrowed Opel in which I could not locate the headlight switch. I thought the whole thing very cultural. The best bits of it were like that.

I spent my days gutting a house, and did it immensely poorly. After I'd left, the whole edifice began to sag dangerously and I know in my heart that that was somehow my fault. I was so useless at the renovations gig that I'm not at all sure how I screwed it up. I just know I did. There was a lot of random swinging of a sledgehammer.

Erik and his wife, Karin, adapted their routines around me. The kids—aged eight, six and two—were fascinated at first. Every single day, the oldest, Jacoba, asked me, "Has you girlfriend?" She was newly disappointed every time I said, "No. Not since yesterday."

Pitied by children. This was low.

Eventually, I became invisible to them. Erik and Karin lived in a bucolic village about forty-five minutes outside Brussels. It was a pretty, sterile place, unused to bohemians who invited strangers to pop by for months at a time. The neighbours would cross the street to avoid saying hello to me. Which was disappointing because "Good day" was the only thing I could say in Flemish.

I'd set up house in the attic of the half-ruined home, dragging up a mattress and laying out a few books. The windows had been blown out and not yet replaced. At dusk, I'd lie across the sill and stare out across the back of the property, which led to infinite unplanted fields. The sky was impossibly high. The sun never seemed to fully set.

I'd spent most of my life feeling out of place, but this was the first time that seemed like the appropriate response. There was some comfort in that.

Days bled into one another without very much happening. Halfway though the summer, a new refugee arrived—Frans.

Frans was a local with artistic pretensions who came from money. He'd blown all of it trying to bring the Jim Rose Circus—a collection of freaks who enjoyed a very small window of renown in the early 1990s—to the country.

I don't claim any insight into the Belgian mindset, but I think I can say with some authority that they are not especially fond of freaks.

If I was drifting, Frans was utterly lost—bankrupt and broken. Erik put him to work retiling the slate roof of a barn.

I would charitably call myself an unskilled labourer. Frans was more of a furiously ambitious saboteur. When he started on the roof, it seemed to my untrained eye in a state of middling repair. By the end of several weeks, it looked as if a brickworks had been dropped on it from a great height. Imagine Dresden after the firebombing.

Frans would spend the day shuffling about on top of the barn, clinging desperately to the apex because he insisted on working in rubber-soled, patent-leather creepers. It is a Lourdes-level miracle that he didn't fall to his death.

Frans was another Belgian who refused to speak to me. The first time we met, I stuck out my hand, but he just stared at it.

"Frans is having a difficult time," Erik said. Frans—a shambling middle-aged man wearing far-too-fashionable eyeglasses for a roofer—was standing there when he said it. He nodded mournfully in agreement. He spoke English, but refused to do so in my presence. Yes, absolutely. Very difficult.

Frans and I would spend our lunch break together in the backyard that linked the two houses, sitting under a sun umbrella, drinking beer and staring off silently in opposite directions. I consoled myself with the idea that it wasn't just me—Frans hated everyone.

The three of us did enjoy one epic night out after Frans had finished his "work." The evening started in an abandoned theatre. It ended with Frans passing out drunk in a twenty-four-hour diner. One moment, he was mumbling in Flemish. The next, he was face-down in his omelette. He had had the foresight to take off his glasses the second before he went down, and to lay them on the table. Erik was speaking to me as it happened. Without breaking eye contact, he reached over, grabbed Frans by the hair and gently laid his head back against the banquette.

Once Frans had regained a very few of his wits, we set off to find his car. I looked at Erik, alarmed. He was doing his Nazi smoking thing.

"We're not going to let Frans drive, are we?"

Erik waved his cigarette around thoughtfully and said, "It's his car, *non*? I suppose we must."

Well, if we must.

When we got to the automobile—one of those low-slung half-car, half-truck European deals—Frans began wrestling with the front seat so that I could slip in the back. Once I'd done that, he went to the other side and began yanking on the other seat. We left him to it until he realized there were only three of us. I suppose the hope was that the struggle might sober him up a bit.

Then he dropped his keys and toppled over trying to pick them up. I recall the sound of the top of his head hitting the pavement.

I have been really, truly afraid perhaps a half-dozen times in my life. That kamikaze ride through the centre of Brussels as the sun began to rise was one of them. Frans ran reds. He mounted curbs. He glanced a light post. Had there been anyone else on the road, you'd have seen the resultant carnage on CNN.

Despite the fact that it was just after 5 a.m. and perhaps one and a half of his five senses were still operational, Frans wanted very badly to go to an outdoor flea market. Again, I gave Erik the look. Again, Erik gave me the "I suppose we must" shrug. The whole thing had a very bad, last-twenty-minutes-of-*Das Boot* feel. And not just the smoking.

Frans found a parking spot near the market. There may have been fifty feet of open curb, yet he insisted on backing into it. He hit reverse like Goggles Paisano and slammed into the car behind him, knocking off its bumper. Then he rammed it into first gear and shot forward the other way, hitting the car in front of him as well.

Frans opened the driver's side door and fell out in slow motion. Lying on the pavement, he remained momentarily curled in the posture of someone sitting behind a steering wheel. He even had his arms stretched out in front of him.

Erik picked Frans up and he stumbled toward the market. People had begun laying out their goods on blankets in a cobbled square. Frans tromped through them, heading in a straight line for a stuffed boar's head.

The last I remember of Frans is seeing him standing ankle-deep in the midst of some unamused vendor's wares, trying to purchase the boar. Frans was cunningly reducing his price at each pass. The salesman kept repeating the same number—"1,500 francs."

Erik and I stood to one side, staring dully.

"This is foolish," Erik said and we left in a hurry lest Frans notice us and insist on more driving. I never did find out if Frans got his pig, or if he survived for that matter.

At that point, the summer was winding down and I was anxious for some sort of catharsis. I hadn't learned anything in particular or had any of the revelations I'd hoped for. I'd done one terrible draft of a film bible, which Erik—again, I have an easier time believing Area 51 is a thing than that this actually happened—paid me for.

We'd tooled about the country a bit. I'd visited Leuven and Bruges. One night, we ended up in a brothel in Antwerp. The next morning, Karin turned to me at breakfast and announced brightly, "So I hear you visited the hookers!" I spit coffee across the table and the children applauded.

The last hurrah before I set off for . . . well, I had no idea where I'd go from there . . . was a music festival up by the Dutch border. It was a two-day gig. Karin would go with me on the first day; Erik on the second.

I tried to pay for my ticket, but they wouldn't have it.

A few days earlier, Karin and I had gone to see Baz Luhrmann's *Romeo and Juliet*. On the street afterward, Karin stopped suddenly, blurted out, "It was so beautiful," and burst into tears. I stood there rubbing her shoulder while she cried. She snuffled into the arm of her coat for a long time, hiding her eyes like a child. It was raining. I had no idea what was really going on, but I'll never forget it.

"You paid for my ticket to the film," Karin said. And while I had, it was about a twentieth of what the concert would cost them. What could you do with people like this? I mean, seriously?

In the total summation of your life, you may vividly recall forty or fifty days. Maybe. I'm forty-four as I sit here and I've got about twenty that stand out. Those two days at the concert—the name of which, like so many of the small details of things that have happened to me I've completely forgotten—were like that. I can think back and smell the smells.

It isn't so much what happened, but how I felt about it happening. There was a heightened sense of switching on the mind's internal "record" button, so that a moment could be captured and revisited for reference—"This is what it feels like to be young."

There wasn't anything special about the concert itself— thousands of people, a few dozen acts, too many booze tents and a farmer's field of steadily deteriorating condition. The Prodigy headlined the first night (loudly). Bowie closed the second (magnificently).

Erik and Karin were the sort of people who knew everyone. They could not go anywhere in the country—a bar, a grocery store—without running into one person who was one other person removed from some good friend of theirs. So if there were 150,000 people at the concert, Karin might have known half of them somehow.

It had never before occurred to me that one person could have so many friends. And that all of these friends could be so roundly delighted to see them. It may sound silly to you, but for me it was a small epiphany. I remain baffled and delighted by people who can hold more than four or five people in their circle at any given time.

The venue was set up in an L shape. At either extreme end, there was a stage. At the bend in the elbow, the tent city of beer halls. We ignored the music on that first day.

(Karin did have a visceral reaction to the appearance of Pulp—a band I could not tolerate. She ran up to the front with me trailing behind. When the crowd thickened, she began to push. When it closed up in front of her, she began to shove. "I think we've gotten as far as we can get," I said. She smirked at me, lowered her head and began to burrow into the wall of people. Someone well in front yelped as Karin hit him. Hard. Her head finally popped back up in the front row. She turned back in my direction and waved delightedly. I have always admired viciousness in women.)

But for the most part, Karin stood in one place and received visitors. I fetched the beer and nodded agreeably whenever introduced. I took some pride in the fact that, for the first time, a few people turned to me and began speaking in Flemish. Right at the end, I had begun to blend in.

On day two, I returned with Erik and the pattern was re-established. He stood in one spot, smoking, while people lined up for "Hellos." Then it happened.

We spend our lives sifting through culture. It's hitting us every day, all day long—new things to see or hear or read. We absorb a great deal at the beginning, but our hide gradually thickens against new ideas and experiences.

In my middle twenties, I was very near the end of my beginnings. Fourteen—or six, or eight, or eleven—seemed an awfully long way off. I was already becoming what all of us become—a nostalgist for my own life. Nothing was ever again going to sound as powerful and revelatory as the first time I'd heard The Smiths or lived through the first playoff run or read Tolkien for the first time.

That day may have been the last time something moved me so deeply that it changed the internal calculus of my tastes.

Erik and I were standing in the midst of a crowd of people. I was on my fourth or fifth beer, in the pleasant stage of buzziness. I couldn't understand what was being said, but was enjoying being adjacent to all of this amity. Everything in my world was pretty perfect in that moment.

Then Radiohead came on.

Radiohead was a band my younger brother, Brendan, liked. I knew a song or two, but I wasn't a particular admirer. For me, they were just another noisy guitar-based British pop band. In the late nineties, the musical landscape was littered with them.

Plus, it is impossible to really love anything your brother has discovered first. It'd be like walking up behind Amundsen and saying, "I'm going to plant my flag right here. Beside yours."

It was mid-afternoon. Radiohead had just released *OK Computer*. They clearly weren't yet a very big deal in this corner of Europe—hence the daytime slot.

They opened with "Paranoid Android"—a meandering, electronic dirge that hit me from the first few notes like a falling piano. I had never before (or since) heard anything quite like it. Every time you hear for the first time a song you will never forget, there is the vague impression that you've heard it before.

When I imagine how a scientist experiences his eureka moment, this must be it. That you knew something all along but have only now consciously accessed it. In that sense, the experience of the truly new is not so much a discovery as an unveiling. You've spent your life waiting for this little show to begin. And then the curtain pulls back.

I remember turning slowly on my heel toward the stage and standing there, fixed dumbly to the spot. The band was a long way off. I couldn't see them very well. Was anybody else feeling the same thing I was feeling?

They were. Erik and his friends had stopped talking. They were also staring. Everyone was being struck the same way at the same time, which amplified the effect of wonder.

Erik looked over at me and said, "Maybe we should go closer, *non*?"

For the first hundred or so yards, there was no resistance. Then, once again, the crowd thickened. Erik was no Karin—no burrowing. We got to a comfortable spot about a football field from the stage and stopped. The crowd filled in behind us. This was now a proper crush.

We stood there for a bit, blissfully. Then someone in front of us opened the umbrella.

The day was comfortably warm and overcast. No beating sun. No imminent rain. It's likely that the improbability of the umbrella was the reason no one reacted to it for a while.

The umbrella was blue and huge. Not any normal umbrella, but one several sizes larger than a golf umbrella. More of a beach umbrella, really—at least six feet across.

The umbrella was directly in front of us, entirely obscuring the stage for dozens, possibly hundreds, of people. I couldn't see who was holding it, but knew to a certainty that it was a man. Only a guy could be this stupid.

The crowd on hand was largely Dutch—which meant tall, attractive, buck-toothed and unusually tolerant. What might have caused a short-order riot in many other parts of the world elicited no response for a very long time here. People stood there hoping the umbrella would go away on its own. It did not.

After a minute or so, the grumbling started. That went on for a while. The umbrella remained.

A few people shouted. No effect.

Someone tried yelling in English, just in case. Nothing.

Erik was beside me. Having finished his cigarette, he dropped it dejectedly to the ground, sighed so loudly I turned, looked at me like a man going over the top and said, "*Allez.*"

He sprung through the crowd with alarming violence. Someone would surely have fallen to the ground were we all not so tightly packed together. He split the crowd so that I could now see Umbrella Man about half a dozen yards ahead.

Erik grabbed him by the shoulders and spun him round. He was young and nondescript. He held the shaft of the umbrella primly against his body. I remember very specifically that his mouth was spread in a cartoonish "O" of surprise.

Erik held Umbrella Man there for a moment. Then he reached out and yanked the umbrella away from him. People were pushing away from the commotion, anticipating a brawl. That gave Erik the room he needed to drop the umbrella to horizontal and close it. I was impressed by the fluidity of the motion. I've never closed an umbrella without a fight.

Once it was closed, Erik handed the umbrella back to Umbrella Man—a rough gesture that in movies would have involved a sword and some sort of surrender. Umbrella Man genteelly received his umbrella. Erik returned to where I was standing, gave me a little wink and lit another cigarette.

Radiohead's set was still going on, but you couldn't hear it for the cheering. People reached out to slap Erik on the back and shoulders, so hard and so often that he was swaying in place. It was, I thought, a real moment.

Everything quieted and we returned to the show. Then someone said something loudly in Flemish and many people laughed.

As you may have gathered, Erik was not an effusive person. Aside from good looks, that was his primary attraction. But upon hearing whatever had just been said, he began nodding fiercely. His eyes widened. He looked at me and said, "*Ja, ja*. That is true."

"Why? What did he say?"

"He says that now that the umbrella is gone, we all miss the umbrella."

I could feel my brain throb inside my head. It was the most important thing anyone has ever said to me.

The day got loopier from there. In order to get out of the venue, you had to walk a good ways to your car, which was parked with thousands of others in fallow fields.

It was late. We decided to stop for one last beer. The vendor told us that he had to pack up his kegs in a half-hour and that that operation could not be performed until they were empty. So we could drink all we liked for free until then. You can imagine.

When we got back to the car, the lot was almost empty. We sat there awhile to sober up a little. Erik drove a Daihatsu—a car so small that I could get down on my knees and grab hold of both bumpers simultaneously.

It was very dark out there in the middle of nowhere. Erik asked which direction the exit was in. Having no idea, I pointed to the front. Taking me at my word, Erik drove the Daihatsu directly into a ditch.

The car was so small that neither set of wheels was touching ground, but it was still too heavy to lift. That didn't stop us trying for the better part of an hour.

By then, Erik had decided that we were sleeping there. Perhaps even living there for the foreseeable future. He lay down in the damp grass and gave up.

I could see one light in the distance and I headed that way. It was—and this is what life is like on those rare occasions when things go entirely wrong and you stop caring—a camper van full of Canadian stoners.

I have never known anyone so enthusiastic to do anything as they were to pull that car out of the ditch. Apparently, they'd brought a rope along to Europe for this very purpose. I felt sure they would snap the axle in half or somehow find a way to blow the car up, but it all went off without incident. Then they left.

Eric and I were left standing alone in the field, unimpeded in our journey, the morning sun now becoming a suggestion on the horizon.

That ride home was possibly the closest I will ever come to real peace. I felt that things had been explained to me and that now I understood.

The umbrella and missing it was my life up to that point. I had solved one part of my own mystery. And so, on to the next.